Kol B'Seder Anthology

THE MUSIC OF **JEFF KLEPPER** AND **DAN FREELANDER**

Edited by **Joel Eglash**

TRANSCONTINENTAL
MUSIC PUBLICATIONS
A Division of the American Conference of Cantors

Instructions to download all 113 audio tracks at no charge:
1. Sign in to TranscontinentalMusic.com, **2.** Click My Account, then Digital Library.
or
1. Sign in to TranscontinentalMusic.com, **2.** Search for product number 955029DA and add the Digital Album to your cart.
3. Check out using this unique code: **KBA-LJK6-DF2**
Audio track information can be found on page 239.

Scan the QR code included with each song to listen to Kol B'Seder's original recording!
Please note that some of the original recordings may differ slightly from the printed score.

HEBREW PRONUNCIATION GUIDE

VOWELS
a as in father
ai as in aisle (= long i as in island)
e as in bed
ei as in eight (= long a as in ace)
i as in pizza (= long e as in be)
o as in go
u as in lunar
' = unstressed vowel close to ə or unstressed short e

CONSONANTS
ch as in Bach or Scottish loch (not as in cheese)
g = hard g as in get (not soft g as in gem)
tz as in boats
h after a vowel is silent
r = like the Italian (rolled) or French r

Proofread by Cantor Claire Franco and Cantor Ross Wolman
Copyedited by Debra Corman – Music engraved by Josh Wiczer – Design and compositing by Joel Eglash
Cover design by Sara Streifel and Joel Eglash – Hand lettering by Jocelyn O'Leary

Transcontinental Music Publications Executive Committee:
—Joel Eglash, Cantor Lauren Phillips Fogelman, Cantor Claire Franco, and Cantor Steven Weiss
American Conference of Cantors: President, Cantor Seth Warner; COO, Rachel Roth
TMP/JLicense Customer Support: Stacey Berliner – TMP/JLicense Production Assistant: Eden Franco

TRANSCONTINENTAL MUSIC PUBLICATIONS
A DIVISION OF THE AMERICAN CONFERENCE OF CANTORS
The world's leading publisher of Jewish music since 1938
1375 Remington Road, Suite M – Schaumburg, IL 60173
847.781.7800 – tmp@accantors.org

Printed in the United States of America – 10 9 8 7 6 5 4 3 2 1
Item number 994055 – ISBN 979-8-9889024-5-4
Includes unique audio download code insert

TranscontinentalMusic.com – KolBSeder.com

This book is dedicated to our loving and supportive families:

Ruth Klepper

Kenneth Klepper

Deeana Klepper, Liora Klepper; Rachel and Alexandra Klepper

Elyse Frishman, Jonah Freelander and Sarah Perlmeter,
Adam Freelander and Julie Stein, Aviva and Ruben Freelander

In loving memory of those whose steadfast love
continues to touch and inspire us:

Lawrence F. Klepper

Aviva and Robert Freelander

David Jacob Freelander

Devra Hanna Freelander

In memory of our mentors and colleagues
who supported and shaped our journey:

Theodore Bikel

Debbie Friedman

Rabbi Peter Knobel

Velvel Pasternak

Rabbi Robert Samuels

Rabbi Malcolm Stern

Dr. Judith Tischler

הם הם שמראים לאדם את הדרך
They are the ones who have shown us the path

Funding for *Kol B'Seder Anthology*
was generously provided by

SHALOM RAV UNDERWRITERS

Sheila and Loui Dobin
We are proud to have been there at the start of your incredible legacy.
It has been part of the soundtrack of our lives and those of so many others.

The Freelander Family

Adam Freelander, Julie Stein, Aviva Freelander, and Ruben Freelander
Dad—The gifts you've given the world are immeasurable. Your monumental musical legacy makes us so proud. We love you so much. -Adam and Julie
Saba—We love your music! We love you! -Aviva and Ruben

Jonah Freelander and Sarah Perlmeter
Your music and the countless lives it has touched are a tremendous source of pride and admiration for us. We couldn't love you more.

Rabbi Elyse Frishman
Danny—You and Jeff open our Jewish hearts with your music. Your love for song and harmony fills us with joy and connects us. Our family is ever richer for your offerings, and I am ever grateful for your devotion to our people. All my love.

LO ALECHA UNDERWRITERS

Dr. and Mrs. Alexander and Dyan Cohen
Thank you, Danny and Jeff, for being the inspiration for many Jewish musicians over the past fifty years.

Ruth Klepper
To my son Jeff—I am very proud of you and all you have done over these fifty years.

OR ZARUA SPONSORS

The Klepper Family

Dr. Alan Mason

MAH TOVU SPONSORS

Janet Abrams and Steve Pruzan

Barnert Temple, Franklin Lakes, New Jersey

Cantor Joshua Breitzer

Cantor Deborrah Cannizzaro

Cantor Claire Franco and Cantor Ella Gladstone Martin
of The Community Synagogue, Port Washington, New York

Cantor Alan J. Brava and the Free Synagogue of Flushing, New York

Bonnie Denmark Friedman

Stephanie Gertz and Cantor Steven Weiss

Rabbi Rachel Hertzman and Rabbi Rex Perlmeter

Kathy and Dan Kaberon

Cantor Leigh Korn

Daryl Messinger and Jim Heeger

Jo-Ann and Michael Price

Sherie and Arnie Reiter

Deborah Speyer and Rabbi Serge Lippe

Rabbi Shira Stern and Rabbi Donald A. Weber

The Clergy Team at Temple Emanu-El, Dallas, Texas
Rabbi David Stern, Rabbi Debra Robbins, Cantor Vicky Glikin,
Rabbi Amy Rossel, Rabbi Kimberly Herzog Cohen, Cantor Leslie Niren, Rabbi Michael Lewis

Cantor Shanna Zell

MODEH ANI CONTRIBUTORS

Anonymous

Steffi Aronson and Eric H. Karp

Rabbi Cantor Vicki L. Axe

Ayelet Tours

Carol Beyer

Rabbi Gary and Marianne Bretton-Granatoor

Kathleen and Richard Cameron

Rabbi Donald P. Cashman

James and Claire Castleman

Aryell Cohen

Rabbi Fred Greene and Congregation Har HaShem, Boulder, Colorado

Joe and Cantor Kari Eglash

Cantor Kenneth Feibush

Rabbi Michael Feshbach

Cantor Lauren Phillips Fogelman

Prof. Sally B. Frank

Randee and Dick Friedman

Cantor Jennifer Frost and Rabbi Richard Prass

Abby Gilbert

Cantor Elizabeth Goldmann

Barbara Lerman-Golomb and John Golomb

Cathy Goodfriend and Paul Reichenbach

Cantor Gail Hirschenfang

Cantor Rachel Gottlieb Kalmowitz

Cantor Vladimir Lapin

Cantor Barbra Lieberstein

Cantor Jamie Marx

Cantor Fredda and Cantor Jack Mendelson

ONEG Kallah Participants
Rabbi Richard Agler, Dr. Hillary and Rabbi Eliot Baskin, Rabbi Peter Berg, Sue and Rabbi Joe Black,
Patti Gerstenbith, Mike Goldman, Rabbi Sam Gordon, Rabbi Daniel Grooper,
Lori and Rabbi Steven Kaye, Judi Levine, Rabbi Jonathan Miller, Rabbi David Segal

Cantor Barbara Ostfeld

Barbara Pollard, and Mitch and Cantor Laura Stein

Cantor Juval Porat

Cantor David Reinwald

Deborah and Robert Render

Jan Rose

Carol and Rick Rosenthal

Irene Rosenzweig and Rabbi Howard Jaffe

Rachel and Jonathan Roth

Cantor Faryn Rudnick

Cantor Tracey Scher

Cantor Lisa Segal

Cantor Judith Seplowin

Cantor David Serkin-Poole

Cantor Leon Sher

David Shukiar

Brenda Spiegler and Mark S. Anshan

Temple Sinai of Sharon, Massachusetts

Temple Sinai of Sharon Guys Group

Jane and Rabbi David Wolfman

Malka and Cantor Ross Wolman

Cantor Jenna Mark and Woodlands Community Temple, White Plains, New York

---

DONORS

Cantor Lauren Adesnik

Cantor Suzanne Bernstein

Rabbi Amy B. Bigman

EJ Cohen

Ron and Joan Cohen

Cantor David Frommer

Rabbi Arnie and Sarah Gluck

Cantor Rabbi Jon Haddon

Mark Kamins

Rabbi Ellen Lewis

Cantor Barbara G. Margulis

Cantor Jen Roher

Shabbat Evening

Shabbat Morning

Shabbat Morning *continued*

Havdalah

Yizkor

Consecration

Multiple Vocal Parts *continued*

Sermon Anthems and Concert Repertoire

Sermon Anthems and Concert Repertoire *continued*

Preface by Kol B'Seder

WE HAD ALREADY BEEN SINGING TOGETHER for a couple of years when Jeff came up with the name Kol B'Seder, a pun on the Hebrew expression הכל בסדר / *hakol b'seder*, meaning "everything's okay." In 1975, we were expanding from a duo to a band, and every band needs a memorable name. But not even Jeff fully appreciated what he was doing when he replaced the letter *kaf* (כ) with *kuf* (ק).

Changing כל / *kol* (meaning "all") to קול / *kol* ("voice") created a second meaning to our name: "(our) voice (is) okay." Those two words say a lot about who we are and what we have been trying to do over the past half-century.

First, the pun itself: "all" and "voice"—one sound with two meanings—suggests a certain playfulness, a sly wink, and if you have ever seen us perform, you know that not taking ourselves too seriously is an important part of who we are.

Second, the meaning of "voice is okay" is precisely who we are. We're not professional musicians or great singers; we are first and foremost a rabbi and a cantor in the traditional sense. Composing, recording, and performing are what we do "on the side." We are educators and artists whose mission is to create music for Jewish spaces and inspire Jews of all ages to seek deeper meaning in Jewish study and prayer.

This is our third songbook, though it supersedes the previous two (*Songs for Growin'* [ARE, 1992] and *The Kol B'Seder Songbook* [Tara Publications, 1996]). It contains every song we wrote together, plus the vast majority of Jeff's solo compositions. The discography found in the back of this volume lists all of our albums, some of which were originally released on vinyl and cassette and are no longer available; we have consolidated virtually all of our previous recordings onto three compilation albums called *Snapshots*, volumes 1–3. Our latest album, *We Are Partners* (2024), contains thirty of our more recent songs, released for the first time. (This book includes audio tracks for all 113 songs. In addition to Transcontinental Music, our recordings are available at kolbseder.com and all streaming platforms).

Nothing makes us happier than to see and hear people of all ages singing our music. If you are a cantor, rabbi, music director, educator, or songleader, we hope you will explore not only the familiar songs, but the many others included here. The song descriptions found in back will give you some insight into the songs' creation, and the Category Index will help you find songs to fit any given theme. We have also included a streaming audio link (QR code) for every song to enhance the usefulness and enjoyment of this volume.

We regard the printed page of music as a jumping-off point—our recordings are our personal interpretations. We encourage you to experiment and to shape the music to fit your particular needs. We have added some harmony parts to use with volunteer or children's choirs, but the tempo, key, arrangement, and "feel" are totally up to you. (If you are a conductor or choral singer, we invite you to try some of the beautiful choral arrangements of our music published by Transcontinental Music.)

This anthology and recording could not have come to fruition without the leadership of Joe Eglash, director of Transcontinental Music Publications and editor of this book. His professionalism, talent, and passion for Jewish music of all styles has strengthened TMP as he leads it into the future. We are grateful to him for his partnership and vision.

Our approach to worship has been significantly influenced by the thinking of our teacher Dr. Lawrence Hoffman. He helped us to understand our music as a pathway to deeper meaning and greater spirituality in communal prayer. We treasure his friendship and his many insights.

We could not have reached this milestone without the love and support of our life partners, Dr. Deeana Copeland Klepper and Rabbi Elyse Frishman. They are themselves inspiring Jewish leaders and educators whose encouragement and appreciation of our work have contributed greatly to our creativity and success.

With this anthology and our new album, *We Are Partners*, we mark the culmination of our fifty-year journey, a blessing that has far exceeded our dreams or expectations. Just as our songs celebrate the partnership between God and humanity, so do we celebrate with gratitude our partnership, our friendship and collaboration, and the partnership we have always treasured with you, our audience of supporters, colleagues, teachers, friends, and family. Thank you!

Baruch atah, Adonai Eloheinu, Melech haolam,
shehecheyanu v'kiy'manu v'higianu laz'man hazeh.

בָּרוּךְ אַתָּה, יי אֱלֹהֵינוּ, מֶלֶךְ הָעוֹלָם,
שֶׁהֶחֱיָנוּ וְקִיְּמָנוּ וְהִגִּיעָנוּ לַזְּמַן הַזֶּה.

Praise to You, Adonai our God, Sovereign of the universe,
for giving us life, sustaining us, and enabling us to reach this season.

– Jeff Klepper and Dan Freelander
Elul 5784/2024

About Kol B'Seder

DAN AND JEFF MET AS COLLEGE STUDENTS IN 1971. Rooming together as faculty at a Jewish youth retreat, they sang late into the night. Their voices immediately clicked into harmony, and they soon began performing for Jewish audiences.

From their beginning as songleaders and composers of new Jewish songs through their individual careers as rabbi and cantor, Kol B'Seder has helped create a unique canon of American Jewish music. The duo is celebrating the fiftieth anniversary of its most famous song, "Shalom Rav," a Hebrew prayer for peace. It is sung around the world and often mistakenly thought to be a traditional melody.

Kol B'Seder's singing style has been likened to Simon and Garfunkel, combined with the humor of musical comedians such as Alan Sherman and Weird Al Yankovic. For most of the '70s, '80s, and '90s, along with the music of their close friend, the late Debbie Friedman, *z"l*, Kol B'Seder's music defined a new Jewish sound that was both joyous and spiritual. Spread by word of mouth and cassette tapes, their songs became a "Jewish soundtrack" for thousands of youth at camps, schools, and synagogues worldwide. One commentator described them as "the Beatles of contemporary Jewish music."

Kol B'Seder has performed throughout the United States and in Israel, England, and Russia. For many years they appeared annually at the CAJE conference for Jewish educators. In 1978, they sang in Central Park for the Salute to Israel Concert. In 1987, they led the music for Freedom Sunday, a rally in Washington, DC, supporting Soviet Jewry and attended by a quarter million people. And in 2007, they were honored with a special concert of their music by the renowned Zamir Chorale of Boston.

Their music was once considered too radical for the bimah, but over time, their songs became *de rigueur* at many synagogue services. Today, when guitars and synagogue rock bands are commonplace, Jeff and Dan have embraced their role as Jewish educators and spiritual leaders. From "Modeh Ani" to "Shalom Rav," their melodies have given children and adults alike access to Jewish tradition and contemporary spirituality.

Both are now retired, Jeff as a synagogue cantor and college instructor in Boston, and Dan as a former senior vice president of the Union for Reform Judaism and president of the World Union for Progressive Judaism. Their influence on several generations of Jewish musicians, cantors, and Jewish leaders has been profound. Every year Jeff inspires budding songleaders at Hava Nashira, the summer workshop he and Debbie Friedman founded. Dan is on the board of the Zamir Choral Foundation, supporting Jewish choral music for adults and teens internationally, and he coordinates the annual North American Jewish Choral Festival.

For more information about their recordings and history, visit kolbseder.com, or kolbseder.bandcamp.com. Video clips from their concerts and TV appearances can be seen at youtube.com/user/kolbseder.

UAHC Kutz Camp, 1976. (Photograph by Peter Weinrobe)

North American Jewish Choral Festival, Stamford, Connecticut, July 2022.

About Jeff Klepper

Jeff Klepper grew up in New York City and was deeply affected by the popular culture and social movements of the 1960s. His parents, Larry and Ruth, were active in Democratic politics and supported John F. Kennedy for president in 1960, bringing Jeff along to campaign events, where he learned the value of civic engagement. Larry, an attorney, attended the 1963 March on Washington and later took Jeff to hear Pete Seeger, which sparked his lifelong interest in folk music.

Jeff begged for a guitar and set about learning a wide range of folk, blues, and protest songs. While not a musician, Larry Klepper had studied magic as a teenager and enjoyed performing for children, and Jeff's first gigs consisted of playing a song or two at his father's magic shows. Jeff inherited musical talent from his paternal grandfather, an amateur violinist. One of his earliest musical memories is singing Passover songs at family seders. Jeff's family belonged to a Reform synagogue, where Jeff, studying for his bar mitzvah, caught the attention of esteemed music director and composer A. W. Binder, who trained and encouraged him to sing the traditional Shabbat and festival *Kiddush* for the congregation.

By his teens, Jeff was performing songs by contemporary figures like Bob Dylan, Paul Simon, and the Beatles. In 1968, after moving to Albany, New York, he attended a Reform Movement summer camp, Joseph Eisner in Great Barrington, Massachusetts, where he first encountered popular Jewish songs. Quickly absorbing this new repertoire, at age fourteen he became songleader of his NFTY youth group. His synagogue sent him to study songleading at NFTY's leadership institute at Kutz Camp Institute in Warwick, New York, and Jeff spent parts of three summers there, learning how to lead songs from Debbie Friedman (and her teacher, Jim Schulman), which led to him becoming songleader for his NFTY region in central New York State.

Attending college at Clark University in Worcester, Massachusetts, Jeff was introduced to Worcester-born Danny Freelander, who was attending Trinity College in Hartford, Connecticut. Before long, the duo was singing at various Jewish events, and inspired by Debbie Friedman's first LP album, *Sing Unto God*, they began to create music of their own.

Jeff returned to Camp Eisner as songleader in 1972, where he taught and led the new Jewish music now pouring out from Debbie Friedman, Michael Isaacson, and others, as well as his own songs and new Israeli songs emerging from the Chassidic Song Festival.

Jeff and Dan's original songs (most notably "Shalom Rav") began garnering attention in the Reform community as a result of their inclusion on the *Songs NFTY Sings* albums. This and other factors led Jeff to transfer to Hebrew Union College–Jewish Institute of Religion in New York City to become a cantor, beginning his studies in 1974.

It was during his HUC years that Jeff, Dan, and several others put together a Jewish rock band called Kol B'Seder. Jeff and Dan continued co-writing songs, which were "road tested" each summer at the Joseph Eisner Camp, their spiritual home.

While in cantorial school, Jeff also participated in the continuing series of *Songs NFTY Sings* albums, and co-wrote and recorded two albums of Jewish songs for children. He endured his classes at HUC, where (at the time) guitar-playing cantors were not appreciated, preferring to seek out musical collaborations with Israeli, klezmer, and jazz musicians.

After Jeff's ordination in 1980, he and Dan refashioned Kol B'Seder back into a duo, and they recorded their first album, *Shalom Rav: Kol B'Seder in Concert.* In 1981, Jeff was invited to spend a year in Haifa, working with American and Israeli youth at the Leo Baeck Education Center, during which time he wrote a new collection of songs influenced by contemporary Israeli music. These were recorded several years later as Jeff's first solo album, *Yom Chadash.*

Jeff spent the rest of the 1980s and 1990s in Evanston, Illinois, as cantor of Beth Emet the Free Synagogue, where he quickly became part of the fabric of Jewish life in the Chicago area.

Kol B'Seder continued actively recording and performing, releasing four original albums during the 1980s and '90s, performing for synagogue and JCC audiences across the United States, in England, and in Israel. Jeff's cantorate flourished, and his connection to Beth Emet and the late Rabbi Peter Knobel brought great satisfaction. He took classes at Northeastern Illinois University, earning his master's degree in applied vocal pedagogy and performing a graduate recital of Hebrew songs by Paul Ben Haim.

In 1986, he met Deeana Copeland, a graduate student in history at Northwestern University. They were married in 1987, and a few years later their daughters, Rachel and Liora, were born.

In 1991, Jeff joined forces with Debbie Friedman and OSRUI Camp Director Jerry Kaye to create a new program to train Jewish songleaders. Hava Nashira was born the following summer. After three decades the annual program continues, under the auspices of Sing Unto God.

Experiencing the cycles of birth and death—Jeff's becoming a father in 1991 was followed by his own father's death in 1994—led to a creative period in his songwriting that culminated in the 1997 album *In This Place*, which features some of his most intimate songs.

As the twenty-first century approached, there were bumps in the road. Having contended with frequent bouts of voice strain for much of his career, likely brought on by years of camp songleading without a microphone or proper warmup, Jeff's singing and speaking voice began to falter. Seeking medical advice, Jeff was diagnosed with spasmodic dysphonia, a neurological condition that prevents the vocal cords from vibrating correctly and for which there is no cure. He could still sing and continued to do so, though his voice was less reliable, but in spite of the challenges brought about by his condition, Jeff maintained a stoic resolve to continue his life's work.

At the same time, Jeff's wife, Deeana, received an appointment to Boston University, and the Klepper family moved to Boston. Deeana is now a professor of history and religion at Boston University and the author of two scholarly books on medieval history.

As the new millennium began, Jeff kept up a busy schedule of freelance singing and teaching until one of his part-time synagogue jobs, at Temple Sinai of Sharon, Massachusetts, evolved into a cantorial position. Working with a vocal coach, Jeff strengthened his voice well enough to meet the demands of a full-time job. He served Temple Sinai from 2003 until his retirement in 2019 and was named cantor emeritus.

In 2000, he was appointed to the editorial committee for *Mishkan T'filah*, the new Reform siddur, and spent the better part of 2004 editing its sixty-page song section, which included, for the first time, songs in Yiddish and Ladino, along with traditional songs and contemporary songs from Israel.

Jeff's third solo album, *Live in Concert: Jewish Music for the Masses*, was released in 2002. It featured old and new performances, including Jewish-themed parodies of Bob Dylan songs. Dylan and his music has been a topic of endless fascination for Jeff, inspiring him to create an audio-visual lecture called "Bob Dylan's Jewish Blues," which he has presented widely.

In 2003, Jeff joined the faculty of Hebrew College in Newton, Massachusetts, where he continues to teach and coach students in Jewish music and guitar. In 2007, he was honored by the Zamir Chorale of Boston with a special concert featuring choral arrangements of his music, at which he was joined by Dan Freelander.

Now several years into retirement, Jeff enjoys the more leisurely pursuits of walking, reading, listening to music, playing (and teaching) guitar, and studying the mandolin. He is looking forward to digitizing cassette tapes of old performances, writing his memoirs, and spending time with family and friends.

* * *

Introduction by Jeff Klepper

It all began at camp. The year was 1968 and the place was Great Barrington, a little town nestled in the Berkshire Mountains of western Massachusetts. It was a Reform Movement summer camp called Joseph Eisner, and I was about to spend a month away from home for the very first time.

That summer was life-changing. At age fourteen I was a tall skinny kid, armed with a brand-new twelve-string Guild guitar, a birthday present from my parents. Since fourth grade, I had learned to play every song I could figure out from the folk music records we had around the house by singers like Tom Paxton, Judy Collins, and my hero, Pete Seeger. Even before I strummed my first "D" chord in 1962, folk songs had become the center of my world. Folk music was huge in the early sixties, and groups like the Kingston Trio and Peter, Paul, and Mary regularly rose up the pop charts.

All it took was a day at camp to realize I had entered another world, where singing ruled the day. The songs and blessings we sang after every meal were mostly in Hebrew, and while many were unfamiliar, the melodies were simple and easy to learn. And learn them we did—we sang them until our voices gave out, and we couldn't wait for the next day to learn another song and sing some more.

But what really captured my attention were the songleaders, and I spent a lot of time watching them. They were the conductors of this musical madness, the rock stars of camp, able to raise their guitars in the air and, through sheer charisma, cause the rafters to shake with the sound of hundreds of voices.

I quickly saw that the guitar was not just a maker of music, it was a scepter of sound, a symbol of great power, a power for good. I had seen this phenomenon already at Pete Seeger concerts, where thousands of strangers swayed back and forth, singing "Michael Row the Boat Ashore" and "We Shall Overcome" in harmony, and here was the same musical energy being used to create *k'hilah k'doshah*, a sacred community at camp!

After a couple of days it became apparent that the camp program was structured around musical rituals. From sunrise until lights-out, everything revolved around singing. Every morning before breakfast we gathered at the flagpole to raise the US flag and sing a patriotic song. Blessings before and after every meal were sung, of course, with a few silly wake-up songs after breakfast, a quick twenty minutes after lunch, and a half-hour of singing after dinner.

There was a brief morning service every weekday, and each unit had a daily music class for learning the basic camp song repertoire. In the evening, there might be a talent show or campfire with yet more singing, and the day was not done until one of the songleaders visited our bunk for "cabin prayers," which consisted of tranquil songs like "Sounds of Silence" or "Leaving on a Jet Plane." These and many other contemporary folk songs became instant classics, yet we could hardly imagine the influence they would have on the Jewish camp song repertoire just a few years later.

As I've said, most of the songs we sang after meals in the dining hall were completely new to me, but at least they were simple, with one or two Hebrew lines, and many of them had harmonies and hand motions. The songleader in charge would stand at a single microphone while one or two assistants would stroll around the room with their guitars, singing and smiling and trying to cajole the masses to follow along. Song sheets were useless in the dining hall, where they would be torn and ragged after a single day, so the songleaders painted lyrics on sheets of butcher paper and hung them around the room.

The songs of Shlomo Carlebach, while immensely popular in more traditional circles, were just starting to cross over into the Reform Movement with songs like "Am Yisrael Chai" and "Esa Einai." Few outside of the Orthodox world knew who Carlebach was, but his songs were certified Jewish hits—simple, catchy, and repetitive, just perfect for clapping and dancing. Chasidic music was catching on in religious schools and camps, and Carlebach's tunes represented the first significant flowering of Jewish American folk-style music.

But during that '68 summer at Eisner Camp, nothing was more popular than several songs written by a young musician named Michael Isaacson. Michael was raised Orthodox in Brooklyn and later studied composition at Juilliard. While attending a workshop in Jewish creative arts at Eisner, he had the idea of writing liturgical songs in the camp style, but with a more sophisticated melodic and harmonic structure. His early songs, such as "L'chah Dodi" and "Ahavat Olam," mashed together musical genres in a way that had never been heard. At first listen they might be mistaken for Israeli songs but with a strong rock beat, a wider vocal range, and chords borrowed from jazz. Years later, as a successful composer in Hollywood, Isaacson looked back on his songs of this period as relatively insignificant, but it is undeniable that he opened the gates. And it wasn't long before Debbie Friedman, Craig Taubman, and many others marched right through behind him, into a new era of American Jewish popular song.

After several days the first Shabbat arrived, and it changed my life forever. At around four o'clock the counselors told us to shower and dress in our Shabbat whites. An hour later, the counselors had us wait in front of our cabin, which was on a hill, the highest point in camp. We were all squeaky clean, looking almost angelic in our white clothes. We could hear the faint sound of music in the distance, and within a few minutes we could see other groups of campers walking through the camp, led by the songleaders, also dressed in white, singing "Mah Yafeh Hayom, Shabbat Shalom," an Israeli song from the 1950s.

Our counselors, several of them also playing guitars, led us down the hill to join the others at the center of camp. There we congregated, our size growing to several hundred, continuously singing, with "Mah Yafeh Hayom" segueing into "Bim Bam," segueing into "Hineih Mah Tov." We were now a mob, a slow moving blob of Jewish kids, being led by a dozen or so guitar-playing counselors. The scene was hypnotic, our steps falling in sync to the rhythm of the songs as we slowly marched to the outdoor chapel for our *Kabbalat Shabbat* service.

It was my first real Shabbat, feeling completely different compared to lighting candles at home and having dinner with my family. We were a wandering tribe of campers, counselors, songleaders, rabbis, and camp staff, celebrating being Jewish in the Berkshire Mountains, under the setting sun of western Massachusetts. Being a shy first-time camper, I was walking by myself, but as I looked around I noticed small groups of kids glomming together holding hands, talking, laughing, singing. I could see the older campers flirting, wishing each other "Shabbat shalom" and leaning in for a quick kiss. I was walking alone, but I wasn't lonely. I was with my tribe, singing our songs, welcoming Shabbat. It felt perfect. I was home.

After services and dinner, the singing seemed to last forever, complete with spontaneous dancing around the tables, sometimes even on top of the tables. The counselors would have to yell at the kids to "get down!" Everyone was drenched in sweat, especially the songleaders. They didn't mind, as Friday was the highlight of their week. How did they do what they did? How were they able to turn a rowdy group of five hundred Jewish kids into a sweaty mob of Shabbat-crazed singers and dancers? I was determined to crack the code. The next Shabbat, I carried a small notepad and pencil and made my way to the front of the room where I could observe them closely, writing down the set list, the keys, the chords, and everything they said. I was hooked. I saw my future.

More than fifty summers have passed since that summer of '68. The world is very different. Thousands of campers, dressed in their Shabbat whites, have walked those same paths and sung those same songs. A few of the old tunes can still be heard, but many have long since been replaced by newer songs. And that is how it should be, as each generation decides what to hold onto, what to let go of, and what to create anew. That's what tradition is all about. Camp will always be a magical place, and the songs we sing are a big reason why.

– Cantor Jeff Klepper
Elul 5784/2024

(Photograph by Ken Berman)

About Dan Freelander

Rabbi Daniel Freelander's life grew from within the rich landscape of music, family, and Reform Judaism. His paternal great-grandfather Hillel was a *chazan*, coming to Burlington, Vermont, from Lithuania in 1881, making his way to Ithaca, New York, and then to Worcester, Massachusetts in the late 1890's. His father, Sonny, was raised in a home committed to Reform Jewish values. After serving in World War II and experiencing the devastation of war, Sonny opened a toy factory and hired workers with physical disabilities, demonstrating their value as productive members of society. Danny's mother, Aviva, after serving in the Palmach during the War of Independence, emigrated from Israel to Worcester in 1950 as a *sh'lichah*. Sonny and Aviva met at an ice-skating rink and fell in love.

That love included a deep devotion to Israel and Judaism permeating Danny's home. Four days a week of afternoon religious school immersed him in Hebrew, and biannual trips to Israel to visit grandparents gave birth to Danny's devotion to Israel.

Danny attended several Jewish summer camps: Avoda, Yavneh, and the URJ Eisner and Kutz camps. The power of communal Jewish singing instantly drew him in. Broadway musical recordings filled his home with songs that transformed stories into experiences. He participated as a choral singer in the synagogue choir, the public high school chorus, and the Massachusetts All-State Chorus. In synagogue and high school, he performed in many musicals. He was a member of a Jewish musical trio called the Neftones, whose repertoire included the music of Peter, Paul and Mary, Phil Ochs, Israeli tunes, and Broadway melodies.

Meanwhile, Danny grew into leadership. Active in the Temple Emanuel youth group, he was encouraged to become a regional officer of NEFTY. Under the mentorship of Deborah Lipstadt, then NEFTY director—she was a second-generation Holocaust survivor and raised in a more traditionally observant background—Danny gained perspective on *K'lal Yisrael.* This appreciation of the larger Jewish people would inspire him to shape music that would touch all Jews.

Attending Trinity College in Hartford, Connecticut, Danny was active in Hillel, student government, and music performing groups. Studying voice with Cantor Arthur Koret at the Hartt College of Music, Danny learned traditional *nusach* and Jewish art music. He taught weekly at Temple Beth Israel in West Hartford as the elementary grade music teacher and confirmation class teacher. There he recognized the banality of many Jewish tunes for children: "Make a matzah pat pat pat. Do not make it fat fat fat…"

At a religious school teacher conference in the fall of 1971, Danny met Jeff Klepper, a student at Clark University in Worcester. In June of 1972, they drove out to Denver for the Rocky Mountain Curriculum Planning Workshop; along the way, they listened to dozens of music cassettes, singing harmonies, and imagining what Jewish music might become. They arrived in Denver ready to team up musically. Following the conference, they recorded their first record of short Jewish songs, including known Hebrew favorites such as "Bim Bam" and "Hineih Mah Tov," all for children. Their paths continued to align at NFTY regional youth conferences. They began composing new Hebrew songs for children and teens to be taught in their respective religious schools and at youth conclaves.

Anxious to get out into the world, Danny graduated in three years with degrees in vocal music and religion. He moved to Boston in 1973 to serve as the cantorial soloist at Wellesley's Temple Beth Elohim and as Hillel counselor at Wellesley College.

Jeff had also moved to Boston. They spent several evenings a week writing new Jewish music. In March 1974, at Brandeis University, they gave their first official performance, premiering their melody for "Shalom Rav." A Mount Holyoke student who knew Jeff from Camp Eisner was sitting in the audience and remarked to her sister the next day, "I've met the man I hope to marry." Elyse Frishman and Danny were married in 1978.

In the summer of 1974, Danny joined the staff of Eisner (with Elyse and Jeff). Four summers alongside talented and visionary new friends taught Danny the finest programming and leadership skills. In this exquisitely creative environment, dreams took shape. He and Jeff would stay up for hours after the camp had gone to sleep, writing new songs that were introduced at lunch the next day. If a piece was sung a second time, it was a hit. In this Jewish Petri dish, programming for the entire camp gave Danny amazing opportunities to brainstorm and experiment in ways that influenced youth and adults for a lifetime.

Though his parents hoped he'd take over the family toy business, Danny's heart was on fire for the Jewish people. He would be a rabbi, able to shape experiences and build sacred communities in the greater Jewish world. He attended the HUC-JIR rabbinical seminary in Jerusalem and New York from 1974 to 1979.

Throughout, Kol B'Seder was central to his life, with weekly rehearsals, dozens of concerts, countless bar/bat mitzvah and wedding receptions, and extensive travel. During his rabbinic training, he also served as WEFTY regional youth advisor and then as a rabbinic intern for NFTY.

Upon ordination, Danny became assistant director of NFTY. Knowing the powerful impact of music on teens and recognizing that a new genre of Jewish folk music was exploding in popularity, he began codifying that music into songbooks for its camps and youth regions. He helped produce several seminal albums in the *Songs NFTY Sings* series. The new music spread feverishly throughout the nation.

Camp and NFTY teens grew into synagogue adults, and they were ripe for Danny's visionary leadership. He was on a mission with his profound love for the Reform Jewish community. So in 1982, Danny became the regional director of the UAHC's New Jersey–West Hudson Valley Council, a position he held for ten years. He supported fifty-eight Reform congregations and their rabbis, and two NFTY regions, JFTY and CNYFTY. He helped birth several new congregations. Danny loved this service, inspiring true Jewish renewal and engagement: commitment to healthy congregational leadership, meaningful Jewish education, uplifting musical worship, and active social justice. It required tremendous dedication and it was fun.

Throughout, he expanded his musical involvements. Within the UAHC, he served as one of four editors of *Shaarei Shirah (Gates of Song)*, an important publication for synagogues containing communal worship melodies. He sang with the Collegiate Chorale at Carnegie Hall, and he traveled and performed widely throughout the country with Kol B'Seder. Continuing to write songs, Danny and Jeff produced three new albums during this period.

Danny's wife, Elyse Frishman, was ordained in 1981 and began her career as a congregational rabbi in Danny's UAHC region. When she became editor of the Reform Movement's new siddur, *Mishkan T'filah* (CCAR Press, 2007), Danny served on the committee; their shared vision of participatory worship helped shape the paradigm of the siddur's layout.

Their first two children, Adam and Jonah, were born in 1983 and 1985. In 1987, Danny's brother

David died from AIDS-related illness, and this compelled Danny's commitment to elevating AIDS awareness in a period of ignorance and hostility. Their daughter Devra, born in 1990, was named after David.

In 1987, UAHC president Rabbi Alexander Schindler invited Danny to direct the Commission on Synagogue Music to advance music within the Reform Movement. The commission organized surveys on synagogue music practices, published new collections for congregational singing, and championed the work of synagogue music and the cantorate. It co-sponsored, alongside the Zamir Choral Foundation, the annual North American Jewish Choral Festival. Danny has guided the festival for over thirty-five years, engaging hundreds of youth and adult singers from around North America and Israel.

Danny became the UAHC's director of programs in 1992, coordinating the many departments serving Reform congregations. The UAHC was the central support for Reform congregations, forging new directions in youth and adult education and leadership, synagogue music, conversion, rabbinical-congregational relations, and publications. Danny supervised *Reform Judaism* magazine, the UAHC Press, and Transcontinental Music. Responsible for the UAHC's Biennial Conventions, he transformed the experience, growing participation from two thousand attendees to over five thousand.

Succeeding Rabbi Schindler, Rabbi Eric Yoffie named Danny as the URJ's senior vice president in 2005 and added supervision of the Union's administrative functions to his portfolio. He worked with the partner organizations ACC, CCAR, and NATA to strengthen professional-clergy-lay relations, including stronger placement processes and salary surveys that helped promote equity. All staff members knew Danny as the go-to person for support. In many ways, Danny embodied the mission of the URJ.

In 2014, after thirty-nine years at the UAHC/URJ, Danny became president of the World Union for Progressive Judaism (WUPJ), the international body of Reform and Progressive congregations. The WUPJ creates and supports progressive Jewish communities around the globe, with headquarters then in Jerusalem and New York. Danny visited dozens of progressive congregations on six continents, strengthening their bonds with one another and helping to integrate their programs with a shared vision and mission. Understanding from his own experience the impact of clergy inspired by NFTY, he championed the Netzer youth movement and the expansion of progressive rabbinic training programs into Russia, Germany, and South America.

Danny and Elyse's sons were married to Julie Stein and Sarah Perlmeter; a first grandchild, Aviva Peach Freelander, was born to Adam and Julie in 2017. Elyse retired in 2017, and they moved from New Jersey to New York City to be closer to their children in Brooklyn. Danny retired on June 30, 2019. Tragically, on July 1, their daughter Devra was killed in a bicycle accident. This profoundly shaped for Danny a deeper commitment to family and toward engaging in further meaningful life work.

In retirement, Jeff and Danny continue a limited performing schedule. They found time to compile and record songs written over the last twenty years of their professional lives. Danny now has time to join and sing with the Zamir Chorale. Danny serves on several not-for-profit committees and boards, including as clerk of the Mary McDowell School for children with special learning needs, the New York UJA/Federation Committee on Israeli Judaism, and Romemu, the NYC congregation to which he and Elyse belong.

Danny is *saba* to his remarkable grandchildren, Aviva and Ruben Dev (born in 2021). They have memorized *Songs for Growin'*, Kol B'Seder's classic 1992 album of children's songs. Through them, and so many others, the music lives on!

* * *

Introduction by Dan Freelander

SINGING SHAPES A COMMUNITY. Our melodies and harmonies blend a sound far holier than we could have imagined alone. Each voice elevates the spirituality of the moment.

When I watch a musical performance, I wonder: How might the performer connect more powerfully with us? What tweaks would make a difference? Would a different tempo or key make the music more accessible? What harmonies are missing? What instrumentation might add to or detract from the moment? Is the performer emotionally present with us?

Creativity for creativity's sake doesn't inspire me, but creativity that unlocks meaning for us does. Artistic mediums are meant to explore the human condition and to have impact and resonate with meaning. I use my voice to encourage powerful musical, spiritual, and communal engagement.

I am proud to have been a part of a "golden age" in American Judaism. I inherited warm and glorious musical and communal traditions that nurtured and welcomed me. My mother would sing to me the *chalutz* (pioneer) songs of her childhood in pre-Israel Palestine. My grandfather would take me to his choral society rehearsals. The synagogue choir and school choruses drew me into the power of choral singing.

Where did I find meaning? In imagining the story lines of Broadway musicals through their record jackets and songs. The songs revealed what the characters were thinking, feeling, and dreaming. I collected the songbooks of these musicals and sat at my piano experimenting with tempo, interpretation, dynamics, and rhythm. How would I sing these songs? I didn't want to imitate the interpretation or performance of the original recording. I wanted to express my own emotion through personal performance and interpretation. I wanted to own the songs, to live the music.

A parallel awareness emerged with the many choral singing opportunities of synagogue life. I disliked singing the melody line. The tenor line harmonies and the full chorus transformed a composition in so many different ways, and I learned the value and importance of the creative interpretation of the conductor. It is the conductor, rather than the composer, who determines how we will experience the music. Choral singing is not about how my particular voice sounds, but how my voice blends with fellow singers to help transform the entire experience. Every performance is a fractal of the original composition. There is no single way to perform or interpret a piece of music.

For me, solo singing is greatly impacted by this principle of choral singing. I want to express the words and music as an honest expression of who I am, not an imitation of the original performer or performance. This pushes me to stretch, regularly adjusting my approach until I find my voice's true resonance with the music. Group singing is the same for me. I search for the missing harmony. This is my creativity, experimenting until I find the "right" note that lifts the music higher for everyone.

So it is that I came to realize how the principles of musical composition, conducting, and singing were principles for leadership and meaningful engagement. These strongly informed my entire professional life. The work with URJ Biennials, NFTY, camps, and congregational leaders focused on creating spiritual communities that deepened our connections to one another and to the Jewish people.

I offer my gratitude to the many musicians, congregational leaders, rabbis, and cantors who encouraged me to create harmonies to their melodies. Chief amongst them are Jeff Klepper, my musical muse, and Elyse Frishman, my guide and life partner. They unlock my voice and give meaning to my life. Each song is rich and expansive because of their love and friendship.

– Rabbi Daniel Hillel Freelander
Elul 5784/2024

Acknowledgments

WE ARE PROFOUNDLY GRATEFUL to each and every individual whose friendship and support have been so meaningful during our half-century journey. It is impossible to list the names of everyone however, and the recognitions that follow represent just the beginning of those we would wish to thank.

To those whose tireless efforts contributed so much to the creation of the Anthology, we are truly grateful:

Joe Eglash
Eric Kilburn
Judith Pinnolis

David Billotti
Cantor Deborrah Cannizzaro
Cantor Claire Franco
Rabbi Elyse Frishman
Jane E. Herman
Rachel Roth
Cantor Steven Weiss

We thank our musical partners who performed with us as Kol B'Seder:

Peter Allard
Peter Bliss
Loui Dobin *
Cantor Mark Elson *
Mitch Gordon
Rabbi Gary Bretton Granatoor
Michael Heimlich
Cantor Barry Kanarek *
Cantor Steve Puzarne *
Steve Samuels *
Steve Zoloto

** Original members of Kol B'Seder*

We thank those whose friendship and support (especially in the early days!) have meant so much to us:

Amy Dattner
Rabbi Deborah Hachen
Jeff Kerne
Rabbi Elliott Kleinman
Michael and Susan Lorge
Paul Reichenbach
Rabbi Donald Rossoff
Eugene Rothman
Rabbi Jeffrey Salkin
Peter Weinrobe

We thank our collaborators; dear friends with whom we have shared musical moments that will live forever in our souls:

Rabbi Joe Black
Doug Cotler
Arnie Lawrence, *z"l*
Howard Levy
Cantor Riki Lippitz
Stuart Rosenberg, *z"l*
Julie Silver
Craig Taubman
Cantor Shanna Zell

We thank our teachers and mentors, whose wisdom and guidance were so crucial in helping us forge our path:

Cantor Lawrence Avery, *z"l*
Jim Ball
Randee Friedman
Joel Grishaver
Rabbi Lawrence Hoffman
Dr. Joshua Jacobson
Rabbi Lawrence Kushner
Matthew (Mati) Lazar
Dr. Deborah Lipstadt
Audrey Friedman Marcus
Rabbi Bennett Miller
Rabbi Seymour Rossel
Rabbi David Saperstein
Rabbi Alex Schindler, *z"l*
Cantor Raymond Smolover, *z"l*
Rabbi Chaim Stern, *z"l*
Rabbi Eric Yoffie
Rabbi Ray Zwerin

We thank our musical colleagues, whose friendship and harmony have strengthened and inspired us:

Cantor Jill Abramson
Ellen Allard
Cantor Dana Anesi
Merri Lovinger Arian
Rabbi Ramie Arian
Noah Aronson
Cantor Josh Breitzer
Steve Brodsky
Rabbi Les Bronstein
Rabbi Donald Cashman
Rabbi Ken Chasen
Dr. Judah Cohen
Aliya Cheskis Cotel
Rabbi Billy Dreskin
Cantor Ellen Dreskin
Steve Dropkin
Rabbi Eric Gurvis
Rabbi Laura Harari
Rabbi Noam Katz
Shira Kline
Rabbi Jon Kraus
Rick Lupert
Chava Mirel
Douglas Mishkin
Rabbi David Nelson
Josh Nelson
Rabbi Lisa Silverstein Nelson
Dan Nichols
Rabbi David Paskin
Rabbi Steven Carr Reuben
Cantor Benjie Ellen Schiller
Cantor Leon Sher
Peri Smilow
Rabbi Andy Vogel
Dr. Rob Weinberg
Cantor Rosalie Will
Rabbi David Wolfman

Introduction by Joe Eglash

It has been, to say the very least, a high point in my career in Jewish music and communal service to have worked on this volume so intimately with Cantor Jeff Klepper and Rabbi Dan Freelander. They are among my favorite songwriters in any genre and have been my mentors, teachers, and now colleagues, for half of my life.

Three years went into creating this volume, which attempts to capture the enormity of Kol B'Seder's impact and influence and collects their 113 songs into one primary resource. From early days debating content and arrangements to intense, long days in the studio co-producing the newer recordings that represent Kol B'Seder's swan song, it has been my honor to help make permanent their unrivaled catalog in a dignified, professional manner.

When I started my career at the URJ and Transcontinental Music in 1998, I searched for a way to emotionally connect to the highly composed Reform music that was worlds away from the *davening* of my traditional upbringing. I became enamored of Kol B'Seder's albums, hearing beloved influences of my own, including Simon and Garfunkel, Pete Seeger, and the Beatles; I heard roots of the American folk music, Israeli music, and Carlebach tunes with which I grew up. The writing felt timeless and classic. Truly, their endless catalog of anthemic songs was what made me passionate about the idea of a career in Jewish music. Today, I remain an adoring fan.

As with all great artists, the appeal wasn't only the art; it was also the artists themselves. Before I got to know Jeff, Danny took me under his wing (as my boss at the URJ) and brought me into this incredible world of progressive Jewish music. Together, we envisioned and carefully planned a new direction for Transcontinental Music, taking TMP from a niche choral music publisher to the world's largest and most important source of Jewish music. We dreamt big, creating books and series that are now considered classic, including *The Complete Shireinu* and the *Shabbat Anthology* and *Ruach* series, which remain in popular use today by Jewish communities throughout the world.

During those years, Jeff and I became good friends, though first I was a fan of his music. I pored over every note not only of the Kol B'Seder albums, but also Jeff's masterful 1997 solo turn, *In This Place*. We bonded over a mutual Dylan obsession and collaborated on numerous projects. I saw the massive influence of his music, his leadership, and his cantorate in every corner of organized Judaism.

That all leads us here. The songs in this book speak of and for *amcha*; they are accessible to every person and to every Jewish moment in our lives. They transcend their deceptive simplicity and give us access to limitless depth. Due to the songs' unpretentiousness and brilliant catchiness, it is no wonder that many of them are considered *miSinai* (of anonymous ancient derivation). It's like the songs have always been with us, gifts from God that capture the Jewish human condition. That is the genius of Kol B'Seder.

You hold in your hands the story of two of the world's most highly influential Jews of the last fifty years. This is the music of true giants of organized Judaism and of all Jewish music. Keep this book close at hand throughout your life, as I will, for its music will continue being the answer.

Hear, O God, when I call with my **voice**. שְׁמַע־יְיָ **קוֹלִי** אֶקְרָא.
(Psalm 27:7)

– Joe Eglash, editor of *Kol B'Seder Anthology*
Elul 5784/2024

Kol B'Seder and Twentieth-Century Jewish Music

By Judith S. Pinnolis

> I think "Shalom Rav" is probably one of the most powerful pieces of liturgical music of contemporary times. Jeff and Danny were looking for ways to involve American Jewish youth in Jewish prayer. And they ended up writing this grand, elegant, regal piece that captures the soul of shalom, wholeness, peace.
> – Debbie Friedman, *z"l*, 2010

In your hands rests a large volume that details the rich, fifty-year history and endeavors of two exceedingly gifted individuals: Jeff Klepper and Danny Freelander. Deeply embedded in a powerful, golden age of Jewish cultural creativity in late twentieth-century America, for years to come they changed the canon of Jewish music.

As Danny and Jeff came of age in this milieu, the Jewish musical world was undergoing a renaissance, bursting with inspiration, innovation, and imagination. The multidimensional space of sounds of its artists—Debbie Friedman, Gladys Gewirtz, Shlomo Carlebach and the Israeli Chassidic Song Festival, Theodore Bikel, Ruth Rubin, and the Yiddish folk heritage—surrounded the young musicians. Also present in this sonic mix were folk tunes and national Jewish music from a nascent Israel; the ever-popular American folk music of Pete Seeger, Bob Dylan, and James Taylor; and synagogue music created by composers Abraham Wolf Binder, Hugo Chaim Adler, brothers Israel and Samuel Goldfarb, and legacy cantors who performed traditional *chazanut*.

When Jeff and Danny started to write songs and discover their voices in the 1970s and 1980s, the success they found was, without a doubt, the result of their talents as well as the influences of the many Jewish musical cultures that were the soundtracks of their formative years. This put their music squarely at the intersection of each of these nodes of Jewish musical expression.

By looking more closely at their lives and musical influences, we can better understand the context for the changes to Jewish music that were a result.

Born into Jewishly active families in the northeast United States in the post–World War II baby boom generation, Jeff grew up in New York City's Washington Heights neighborhood, while suburban Worcester, Massachusetts, was home to Danny. It was an era in which social, educational, and economic barriers fell for American Jews, who were coming of age as a community and beginning to feel truly at home in this country. As a result, many also experienced feelings of liminality, with one foot in each culture.

Both Jeff and Danny were interested in music and studied it from a young age. When he was eleven years old and in sixth grade, Jeff began to study guitar with Harvey Bluetreich, an excellent musician and recent Army veteran who lived in the neighborhood. Bluetreich not only opened Jeff's ears to all sorts of folk music, including the humorous songs of Tom Lehrer, but also gave him an appreciation for the blues and helped steep him in American folk music culture. He taught Jeff fingerpicking in the popular style of Bob Dylan, who was a major musical influence on Jeff at the time. Jeff's repertoire advanced rapidly, and he learned more than a hundred songs with Bluetreich.

Bluetreich did not offer Jeff a traditional classical music education in which he learned from written scores. Rather, his lessons centered on listening and "doing by playing." In this way, Jeff developed a strong ability to learn by ear, which helped him capture the essence of a musical moment and set new songs in the folk idiom. Bluetreich's emphasis also ensured that Jeff memorized a large repertoire of folk and popular music, as well as Yiddish and Israeli songs, giving him a huge lifelong musical vocabulary from which he could draw new musical ideas. In later years, Jeff truly came to appreciate the eclectic musical education he received from Bluetreich.

Jeff's musical journey was also profoundly shaped by the mentorship of Abraham Wolf Binder (1895–1966), the esteemed music director at Stephen Wise Free Synagogue on Manhattan's Upper West Side. Lacking a cantor, it was the synagogue's tradition to have young people sing the *Kiddush* each week at services, and later, those who did were affectionately referred to as members of the "*Kiddush* Corps." Although Jeff lacked any formal musical knowledge at the time, Binder recruited him for the *Kiddush* Corps, patiently mentored him, and even transposed melodies to suit his voice. Jeff fondly recalls his early experiences singing with Binder, which, although challenging at times, helped ignite Jeff's lifelong passion for Jewish music and provided him with his first taste of cantorial singing. In one of his first such experiences, he sang the *Kiddush* for hundreds at a televised interfaith community Passover seder.

Binder's influence on his students went beyond mere instruction. He formed deeply personal connections as he nurtured their young talent. Under Binder's tutelage, Jeff not only discovered his love for singing, but also gained a profound appreciation for Jewish song traditions. Binder's guidance helped steer Jeff to a future as a prominent musician and served as a true testament to the former's power to use mentorship and personal relationships to transform and shape musical legacies.

Danny, on the other hand, had a thorough musical education in piano and voice and learned by reading and practicing from scores, grounding him in different but complementary strengths. From a young age, he could sing by sight and transcribe the music he heard. He also was conversant in Hebrew, since his mother was from Israel, and during summers the Freelanders regularly visited with grandparents and other family members there. His grandfather and great-grandfather were cantors, so he was surrounded by traditional cantorial music growing up and learned *nusach* and *chazanut* from his grandfather. One of Danny's fondest memories is singing the unique family melodies to Passover seder songs that originally were composed by his great-grandfather.

From fifth to ninth grade, Danny sang weekly at services at Temple Emanuel in Worcester, where the Freelanders were members. He knew all the choral responses, first singing as a soprano in the children's choirs and then as a young soloist with a microphone in the synagogue's hidden choir loft. When his voice changed, he sang tenor with the adult choirs on Shabbat and the High Holy Days. Danny also sang in school choirs during high school, including the Massachusetts All-State Choir. In the NEFTY youth group where he was a regional officer, he helped form a pop performing group, the Neftones. Danny's love of choral music and singing in small ensembles stems from this period and continues to this day.

As a result of his synagogue singing, Danny was thoroughly familiar with the music of Hugo Chaim Adler (1894–1955), who had been Temple Emanuel's cantor and music director from 1940 until his death. Danny also was well-versed in the music of other great composers of the classical era of Reform music that was heard and sung in synagogues throughout the late nineteenth and early twentieth centuries.

Classical Reform Music and the *Union Hymnal*

It is possible that the greatest era of Jewish sacred art music composition occurred from 1900 to 1960. At the turn of the twentieth century, the music of a few synagogue composers spread widely through their publications, including the four-volume *Zimrat Yah* (1871–86) by Baltimore-based Alois Kaiser (1840-1908) and *Synagogal Service* (1901), widely known as the "Spicker-Sparger service," jointly published by composer and conductor Max Spicker (1858–1912) and San Francisco Cantor William Sparger (1860–1904). In Mobile, Alabama, organist and choirmaster Sigmund Schlesinger (1835–1906) created *Complete Musical Services—for Sabbath, and the Three Festivals*, a widely popular "Americanized" publication based on a Western choral and operatic style. Edward Stark (1856–1918), son of a cantor and thoroughly grounded in south German *chazanut* yet enamored of Western music, published his influential *Sefer Anim Zemiroth* between 1909 and 1913.

Nevertheless, Reform music remained dominated by the great European composers Solomon Sulzer (1804–90) and Louis Lewandowski (1821–94). Promoted by a cadre of their followers in America, their music became ubiquitous, spreading through synagogues not only because of its artistic quality but also because of print publications, a method of distribution and learning that prevailed before audio recordings. Publications filled gaps caused by a lack of mentorship opportunities for Jewish synagogue musicians. In pre-1900 America, there were only a few cantors and no cantorial training programs in this country, so many synagogues relied on non-Jewish organists and choir directors who could play from printed music.

Meanwhile, immigrants from Eastern Europe arrived en masse in America at the turn of the twentieth century. Among them were cantors with traditional Eastern European *chazanut* training, ushering in the "golden age" of *chazanut* in America (generally considered to be 1880–1930). At the same time, the immigrants sought to adapt to their new American culture and wanted their synagogue music to align with their American experiences. This desire to be "more American," while retaining and incorporating a strong Jewish and traditional core, was a significant factor that helped spur the advent of musical changes that came to be known as "*minhag* America" and were reflected in new melodies and modifications in synagogue worship adopted by the Conservative, Reform, and other liberal movements.

The musical work of Israel and Samuel Goldfarb also came from adapting and mixing cultures: Yiddish and Hebrew, sacred and secular, old-world music and new American melodies. Following their arrival in America in the early 1890s, Israel became the rabbi of Congregation Beth Israel Anshe Emeth (the Kane Street Synagogue) in Brooklyn, and Sam headed the music department at the Board of Jewish Education, also in New York City. In 1918, Israel gained fame as the composer of the *z'mirah* (Sabbath table melody) "Shalom Aleichem," which traveled the world. In the 1920s, the brothers published *The Jewish Songster* in two volumes, which were aimed at all Jews, not only those affiliated with one particular movement.

Following a pattern set in the nineteenth century, many American Jews participated in large choruses, public music events, and other communal gatherings in which singing was used to promote group cohesion and spirit. Group and community singing was an expectation and aim of the Goldfarbs' *Songster*, which was used in schools, camps, clubs, and other Jewish gatherings. Its piano-vocal scores assumed a high level of musical literacy and intended to instill Jewish ideals, texts, and education through music into the general Jewish public. In many ways, the work of the Goldfarbs can be viewed as a precursor to the work of the composers of this volume.

In 1897, Kaiser and Sparger compiled and edited the first *Union Hymnal*, a key document for music in Reform synagogues, to accompany the *Union Prayerbook*. Most of the songs had originated in Western secular music, with composers including Mozart, Haydn, Beethoven, and Rossini, and with European cantors including Sulzer and Lewandowski, although a few traditional Ashkenazi melodies were retained. Hymn lyrics were based on loose adaptations of liturgical or biblical texts in English translation, with some hymn texts by South Carolinian poet Penina Moïse.

Hymns in the 1932 edition of the *Union Hymnal* remained largely choral-based and in four-part harmony, the norm for Reform congregations through mid-century. The team that revised and enlarged the new edition, including Jacob Singer (1883–1964) and Abraham Wolf Binder (1895–1966), endeavored to include hymns with more "Jewish" character. Cognizant of the increasing number of Eastern European Jews coming into Reform congregations, Binder added many melodies familiar and important to them and sometimes also added his own English lyrics. One of his pieces, "Come, Oh Sabbath Day," became a classic.

Although the 1957 edition of the *Union Hymnal* added more contemporary and skilled Jewish composers to the mix, including modernists Jacob Beimel (1875–1944), Heinrich Schalit (1886–1976), Joseph Achron (1886–1943), Pinchos Jassinowsky (1886–1954), and Reuben Rinder (1887–1966), hymns in Reform congregations still were sung formally, led by a professional or trained choir or congregational singing, and usually included organ accompaniment. This style prevailed until the late 1960s and 1970s, when experimentation in synagogue song began.

Subsequent synagogue composers continued to aim to create Jewish choral music that could uplift the soul (*hit'or'rut hanefesh*) and enlighten congregations. The focus was on high art and good aesthetics, based on Western sensibilities. In the opening decades of the twentieth century, many congregations had begun to commission works and support new synagogal compositions, and great compositions of synagogue services emerged. Among them was *Avodath HaKodesh* (1933) by Ernest Bloch (1880–1959). Art composers such as Isadore Freed (1900–60), Herbert Fromm (1905–95), Herman Berklinski (1910–2001), and Max Janowski (1912–91), along with émigrés such as Heinrich Schalit and Frederick Piket (1903–74), elevated the aesthetic and sophistication levels of American synagogue music; a body of work uplifting the best in compositional styles of the twentieth century blossomed. Much of this composed synagogue art music was experimental; some even involved American musical idioms, such as Darius Milhaud (1892–1974) incorporating jazz idioms in his 1949 *Sacred Service for Sabbath Morning*.

The Early Years of Jewish Camping and the Reform Youth Movement

Many Jewish summer camps that began in the late nineteenth century were sponsored by "fresh air" funds and designed to bring Jewish immigrant children and the urban poor out of the cities. Originally, these camps, without specific Jewish content or programming, focused primarily on athletic activities to ensure healthy children. There were some private camps for well-to-do families in this era, but most were philanthropic or ideologically based, often in the Zionist or Yiddishist tradition.

Samson Benderly, who first conceived of summer camping for American Jewish children in the 1920s, saw such camps as a way to "implant a love for and interest in things Jewish and arouse in the child a desire for Jewish knowledge." He felt that an intensive summer study program in Jewish culture, with active, experiential, and hands-on learning could achieve significant results. One of his students, Albert Schoolman, later became the director of Camp Cejwin in the Catskill Mountains, considered to be the first Jewish educational camp in America. By the 1920s, Camp Cejwin had a published songbook for campers.

Historian Jonathan Sarna notes that in the decades that followed, the Jewish camp movement expanded dramatically with the founding of numerous camps: Brandeis Camp Institute in California and Camp Massad in Quebec, both in 1941; Camp Ramah in Wisconsin in 1947; Camp Ramah in the Pocono Mountains of Pennsylvania in 1950; and Olin-Sang-Ruby Union Institute in Wisconsin in 1952. Other camps established in this period include Avodah in 1927, Aguda in 1941, Yavneh in 1944, Lown in 1946, and Sharon in 1946.

In a perceptible shift from the ideological emphases of earlier camps, the camps created in the 1940s and 1950s focused on denominational identities and came under the sponsorship of one of the Jewish religious movements or Jewish cultural institutions. They were committed to Jewish culture and education and devoted to building campers' Jewish character and knowledge. When the Conservative Movement's Ramah camps and the Reform Movement's Union of American Hebrew Congregations (UAHC) camps expanded during the 1950s, their denominational identities had a tremendous impact on the Jewish summer camp experiences of an entire generation of American Jews. From among their ranks came a new cohort of Jewish clergy, educators, scholars, and lay leaders, including Danny and Jeff.

At Reform Movement camps, the serious involvement of rabbis meant these camps placed much more emphasis on promoting spirituality than most other Jewish educational camps. Religious activities were described as the most successful single facet of camp life and brought forth an informal mode of camp worship. This new focus on "informal education" developed as a meaningful addition to supplemental Hebrew and religious school education, not only making camp special but also giving it staying power in the lives of campers long beyond the summer. Communal singing that was integrally woven into religious encounters and personal experiences was vital to creating successful group activities with spiritual components that actively taught concepts and language and promoted Jewish feelings of belonging. As a result, Jewish camps came to play a tremendous role in the mid-century changes that occurred in Jewish synagogue music and ultimately in the Reform Movement as a whole.

Much of this change was embodied in the work of Cantor William Sharlin (1920–2012). Raised in an Orthodox home, Sharlin was a member of the first cantorial class of Hebrew Union College–Jewish Institute of Religion (HUC-JIR) in 1951 and, after buying a guitar, stepped in as music director at a month-long summer camp in New Jersey for disabled children, where he quickly discovered and filled the musical needs of the campers. Shortly thereafter, Rabbi Samuel Cook invited Sharlin to join a NFTY conclave, where he led a few song sessions. In 1952, Cook hired Sharlin to lead group singing at the Union Institute, a newly established Reform camp in Oconomowoc, Wisconsin, later renamed Olin-Sang-Ruby Union Institute. As music leader, Sharlin loved bringing songs—and stories—into the dining hall, where they could boost campers' pride in their Jewish identity and fill the "spirituality gap."

By 1954, Sharlin had moved to California and worked as a summer songleader at UAHC's Camp for Living Judaism in Saratoga, later renamed Camp Swig. Constantly moving around the dining hall, Sharlin taught campers to memorize the songs, erasing the transliterated lyrics he'd written on a chalkboard one by one as the campers learned the songs. He believed that internalizing the words would help them have truly spiritual experiences. Although Sharlin loved Chasidic music, his repertoire in Saratoga was a mix of standard American camp tunes, new civil rights songs, and a few Hebrew liturgical melodies. Sharlin relied extensively on the secular folk song collection *Git on Board: Collection of Folk Songs Arranged for Mixed Chorus and Solo Voice* (1950), which promoted civil rights and the American folk song tradition. He believed it aligned with Jewish identity and the social consciousness that had already entered Jewish camping through music and would become prevalent in the heady days of the 1960s.

Sharlin's work was the forerunner of the songleading tradition that would take root in Reform Movement camps, and by 1964 the Union Institute's songbook, known by its Hebrew name, *Shiron*, was being expanded with significantly more Hebrew and Israeli music. These additions signaled the aspiration that campers would acquire more Hebrew fluency, promoted in a folk music style, with texts of a progressive political perspective. Earlier UAHC and NFTY songbooks contained few Hebrew songs. By the mid- to late 1960s, standard American folk tunes were heavily supplemented by Hebrew melodies of Shlomo Carlebach and, after 1967, *shirei Eretz Yisrael* (patriotic Israeli music from the pioneer days of Israel and Labor Zionist camps).

UAHC Kutz Camp, 1975.

Israeli songs were sung in "Israeli Hebrew" with Sephardic pronunciation. As their use became part of the American repertoire, they contributed to the American Jewish community switching from Ashkenazic to Sephardic Hebrew pronunciation. A lag, however, remained between the pronunciation used to sing the Israeli and new secular songs and the standard liturgy, which clung to Ashkenazic pronunciation. This discrepancy was reflected in the widespread volumes of *The Songs We Sing*, edited by Harry Coopersmith and published by the United Synagogue Commission on Jewish Education of the Conservative Movement. The 1950 volume, which featured complete piano arrangements for each song, transliterated the Hebrew of liturgical texts using Ashkenazic pronunciation and the Hebrew of secular songs using Sephardic pronunciation. This sacred-secular split in pronunciation continued well into the 1960s at Jewish camps but faded rapidly after the Israeli Six-Day War, when Sephardic pronunciation and learning more difficult Hebrew vocabulary became the focus.

In Coopersmith's subsequent publication in 1971, *More of the Songs We Sing*, Sephardic pronunciation dominated, showing the growing influence of Israeli Hebrew, and the piano arrangements were replaced by single lines of music, with chords indicated in lettering above the melody line. This format offered flexibility for informal teaching and options for accompaniment by keyboard or guitar. The score presentation method was also popular in publications for American public schools, demonstrating alignment with public education methods of the time.

During this same era, a new festival in Israel, the Chassidic Song Festival, focused on songs based on common liturgical texts familiar to American Jews. Danny recalls that people wanted to hear more Hebrew and to sing it. The aftermath of both the 1967 Six Day War and the 1973 Israeli Yom Kippur War, as one of the originators of the Jewish camp song movement, Michael Isaacson, has said, "put the nail in the coffin" of using Ashkenazic pronunciation. Following the war, the entire liberal Jewish educational thrust shifted to the Israeli style of pronunciation of Hebrew, and Ashkenazic pronunciation almost completely disappeared.

Both Danny and Jeff attended Jewish summer camps and were active in NFTY as teens. In 1967, at age fourteen, with encouragement from Rabbi Joseph Klein, the spiritual leader of his home congregation in Worcester, Danny attended the Reform Movement's Eisner Camp in Great Barrington, Massachusetts.

The next year, in 1968, just a year after the Six-Day War, Jeff attended Eisner Camp. Immersed in the voices of several hundred campers singing together, Jeff was mesmerized. At Eisner, he met Isaacson and became infatuated with the college-aged songleaders, whom he viewed as pop stars and pied pipers as they paraded around and led the singing to welcome Shabbat. As Jeff tells it, he would walk ten steps behind the songleaders—including David Altshuler, Jerry Brieger, and Hank Sawitz, later followed by Ramie Arian and Linda Zimmerman, many of whom went on to become rabbis, cantors, and Jewish community leaders—just to "absorb some of their aura." Within a few short years, Jeff was not only an acolyte but a leader as well.

Also in 1968, at the UAHC's Kutz Camp in Warwick, New York, Debbie Friedman (1951–2011) learned songleading skills at NFTY's National Leadership Institute, a program for youth group and regional leaders. There she took courses with Jim Schulman, a Texas-based folk singer and songleader. Schulman broke down the songleading process by drilling every note, word, and chord and urging leaders to pay attention to meaning by adding appropriate hand-clapping, body motions, and other elements to the experience.

In 1969, Jeff and Danny both attended Kutz Camp, but they didn't yet know each other and wouldn't meet for another few years. At Kutz, Danny realized that Isaacson was pushing musical boundaries in songs such as his settings of "Ahavat Olam" and "L'chah Dodi." Isaacson's jazzy "Mah Gadlu" traveled the youth circuit to camps and conclaves, where teens went wild, singing at the top of their lungs, standing on chairs, pounding tables, and adding expressive words and motions.

Friedman also was at Kutz that summer and the next, meeting each day for an hour with a small group, teaching Israeli songs. As they sang, she improvised harmonies and taught those as well. Only the texts were written down, with the music learned by ear. Friedman's new method of instruction played a major role in the musical development in Jewish camps and created a milieu that would deeply influence the music that Danny and Jeff would create.

In 1971, Jeff, a student at Clark University in Worcester, taught music in the religious school at Temple Emanuel, where he encountered Hebrew teacher Aviva Freelander. She suggested he meet her son, Danny, a student in Hartford, Connecticut. Danny, who viewed music and religion as connected and didn't want to choose between them, was studying religion at Trinity College while a performance major at Hartt College of Music at the University of Hartford. One of his vocal teachers was Arthur Koret, the cantor at Emanuel Synagogue in West Hartford and a national figure in Jewish liturgical music. Koret challenged him to learn some *chazanut* and create a senior recital that was half cantorial music and half Italian art song. Finally, in December of that year, Jeff and Danny met at a UAHC teachers' conference; not surprisingly, music brought them together. Before long, they were singing together regularly, and from the start, they harmonized wonderfully. Danny had a soft, high baritone with a lyrical quality that blended well with Jeff's more folky natural voice. Meanwhile, Debbie Friedman was experimenting with creative melodies for prayers based on the liturgy of the *Union Prayer Book*. From the start, her goal was to bring Jewish texts to young people. The English words to the "V'ahavta" prayer became "Thou Shalt Love," one of the first songs she set to music. Her melody captured the meaning of the text and had the character of a lullaby. To many, this and subsequent melodies reflected the influence of Judy Collins and Carole King, with harmonies that echoed the music Friedman knew from American popular music and folk recordings.

Kol B'Seder Band at wedding reception, late 1970s. Left to right: Steven Puzarne, Steve Samuels, Loui Dobin, with Dan and Jeff. (Photograph by Clarence Korker)

Even without knowing how to write musical notation, that same year Friedman composed an entire Friday evening service entitled *Sing Unto God*, recording it with members of her former high school choir in St. Paul, Minnesota. Friedman's music was eye-opening for Danny, and with the release of the *Sing Unto God* album in 1972, he realized that Jewish music could be created with new American rhythm patterns and in an American folk idiom, simultaneously incorporating Hebrew texts in new ways. Friedman's music on that first album attracted him in two ways: It was arranged for choir, an especially great love of his, and it was participatory, creating a spiritual feeling among campers. Danny began to realize that he, too, could do more to change the musical landscape of the day.

The following summer Friedman worked at Olin-Sang-Ruby Union Institute, bringing her songs and songleading skills to the camp. Her most popular songs were catchy and tuneful in ways that compelled campers and staff to sing along. In addition to composing, songleading was Friedman's great gift. She understood how to help campers learn songs, and she would harmonize, something she loved to do, to fill the musical gaps. Friedman had a knack for improvisation and, sensing the emotional and spiritual moment in a group, she would lift the mood higher. She injected humor and antics while teaching but continued to challenge her audience until she felt they had it right.

Meanwhile, Danny and Jeff decided to drive together to Colorado to attend a new and innovative program, the Rocky Mountain Jewish Curriculum Planning Workshop. On the long trip west, they talked and sang together, establishing the foundation of their lifelong friendship. Jeff, an experienced songleader and guitarist, found his musical talents complemented Danny's so well that they envisioned forming a duo. At that workshop, they recorded together for the first time—a short record of well-known traditional songs for Jewish schools.

By then, Friedman's tunes were being sung by Reform Jewish youth across the country, and that summer, her "L'chah Dodi" was recorded along with songs by Isaacson and others for the first volume of the *Songs NFTY Sings* album series, which Loui Dobin produced. Eventually, there would be seven volumes, each with new Israeli songs and new Jewish repertoire written by emerging American Jewish singer-songwriters, including Jeff and Danny.

Influences Beyond the Reform Movement

During Jeff's formative years, he was tremendously influenced by American folk music, especially that of Pete Seeger. This music, with community singing as a cultural signifier, had a long history in the Jewish community through camp settings and Jewish organizational life. Jeff began to absorb and synthesize the worship aspect and spirituality of communal singing along with its do-it-yourself, anti-hierarchical facets. His summer camp experiences—as a songleader on the staff of the UAHC's Eisner Camp, where Danny was a unit head and program director—solidified his impression of communal singing as a way both to engender participation and promote solidly effective spiritual experiences. As a result, the music he created with Danny incorporates traditional and new Jewish styles and texts. Jeff's folk-inspired quality generated through acoustic instruments—guitar, mandolin, and harmonica—offers a warm, intimate feel well-suited to the contemplative and introspective nature of many Jewish liturgical texts.

Pop music, another influence on the duo, features catchy melodies and sing-along choruses that are easy to learn and remember. The two also drew on their knowledge of traditional Jewish music. Blending Jewish, Israeli, and Chasidic elements with contemporary American musical styles of the day featuring catchy tunes and refrains helped make their music accessible and relevant to a wide range of listeners from all backgrounds and observance levels. As fans of rock music, they incorporated this style, too, in their music, with electric guitar, bass, and drums to give it an energetic, upbeat, engaging, and entertaining feel.

Around 1973 the music of Tayku, a Jewish band that included pianist Mati Lazar and his friend, composer David Burger, caught the ears of Jeff and Danny as well. Tayku turned Jewish and Israeli melodies into jazz- and pop-influenced vocal works. As a contemporary Jewish performing group, Tayku's musical arrangements (and their humorous interplay) were extremely influential.

Beyond these diverse musical styles, several individuals broadly influenced the two young men during this period: Max Helfman (1901–63) through the Brandeis-Bardin Institute, Gladys Gewirtz, and Shlomo Carlebach.

The significance of the Brandeis-Bardin Institute and Helfman in the development of Jewish music in America cannot be underestimated. Shlomo Bardin (1898–1976) founded the Brandeis Camp Institute (BCI) in 1941, and from the beginning, music and dance were central components of the curriculum, with exceptional lecturers and Jewish leaders as staff. In 1944, Bardin hired Helfman as BCI's music director. Already a well-known composer and choir director, his tenure at the camp was instrumental to its success.

At the camp's site in Simi Valley, California, Helfman was intent on maintaining a nonsectarian environment. He created new liturgical songs that intentionally avoided worship melodies from the denominational movements. Campers learned the new melodies together, which helped create a sense of shared community in which they could pray joyfully. His compositions bridged the gap between the "old" styles inherent in Yiddish folk tunes, familiar from his days conducting Yiddish choruses, and the "high" cantorial and classical art approach he used for compositions at various synagogues he had served. Helfman's teaching and playing the piano at camp were vital to keeping the music interesting and also allowed for inner voices, counterpoint, and sophisticated harmony.

Just as the Goldfarb brothers had helped democratize Jewish music by mixing and blending disparate styles, Helfman melded a folk element to a more sophisticated liturgical art tradition and brought elements of Israeli folk (or "Mediterranean style") into his choral music, fusing modern musical techniques while keeping the music accessible to the large audience of Jewish laypeople.

Dissemination of BCI music started in the late 1940s when Transcontinental Music Publications published the Brandeis Youth Foundation Series, showcasing Israeli songs in Helfman's new settings. This continued through the work of myriad attendees, including Yehudi Wyner (1929–), Jack Gottlieb (1930–2011), Cantor Charles Davidson (1929–2023), Gershon Kingsley (1922–2019), and Cantor Raymond Smolover (1921–2015), who took the music, along with Helfman's methods and lessons, to other institutions and camps including the denominational camp movements, where they would have a significant influence in the decades that followed.

For example, in the 1960s, Smolover created an Arts Academy camp at the UAHC's Eisner Camp that, for several years, trained composers Max Stern (1947–) and Michael Isaacson (1946–) as well as choral director Joshua Jacobson (1948–) among others. Luminary teachers, including Paul Ben Haim (1897–1984), Isaac Bashevis Singer (1902–91), and Lazar Weiner (1897–1982), who taught Helfman's modernistic choral arrangements of Israeli songs from BCI, also were associated with Smolover's Arts Academy. During Danny's first summer at Eisner in 1967, some of Smolover's students organized choirs for the young campers—Danny among them—and led them in choral singing. Although he was unaware of the unique aspects of the experience at the time, it was another introduction for Danny to new and innovative music at a young age.

In that same era, Cantor Charles Davidson composed inventive and creative services using jazz idioms, and Smolover and Kingsley wrote Jewish rock services. These innovations, encouraged by the musical ideas spawned at BCI, would prove to be a factor in shaping the music of the up-and-coming generation of Jewish singer-songwriters.

Gladys Gewirtz, a key figure at Camp Ramah in Wisconsin, also followed Helfman's teaching model and accompanied camp songs on the piano, enriching them with depth and more complex harmonies. Gewirtz also composed numerous original camp songs, including "Himnon Ramah," the enduring Ramah anthem. Later, she moved to Israel, where in the 1960s she became the director of music at the Jerusalem campus of HUC-JIR. In this role, she worked closely with rabbinical students, introducing them to Reform interpretations of Israeli music and arranging Sephardic and Mizrachi melodies. She and Danny crossed paths at HUC-JIR during his first year of rabbinical school in the mid-1970s, where her innovations included introducing a harpsichord for the chapel music, accompanied by a flute and cello *obbligato*, giving rise to a lighter, airier, and more youthful sound. Her arrangements were published by Sacred Music Press of HUC-JIR as *Selections from the Sabbath and Holiday Services of Hebrew Union College Biblical and Archaeological School, Jerusalem.*

Although not widely understood, the influence Gewirtz and her musical arrangements had on a generation of rabbinical students who then served congregations throughout the United States was a part of the story of how musical tastes changed and how an openness to new and different musical forces for a new synagogue sound would develop in the latter quarter of the twentieth century.

Along with changes happening in Reform synagogues and camps, another stream of influence came from Shlomo Carlebach (1925–94), a rabbi and folk singer who reshaped contemporary Jewish music by infusing it with a neo-Chasidic style. Many consider him the most significant Jewish musical figure of the second half of the twentieth century. His simple yet profound compositions included both wordless *nigunim* (melodies) and songs with texts drawn from liturgy and Jewish teachings. He accompanied himself on guitar, blending styles by adapting a casual American counterculture musical veneer and aura.

Carlebach's music was both accessible and emotional. It transcended denominational boundaries, offering solace and spiritual connection to a generation grappling with the aftermath of the Holocaust. He resonated deeply with liberal Jews in the 1960s, and his influence spread widely in Reform circles, where the melodies symbolized a significant departure from traditional Reform hymns; they fostered a perception of a return to a more "authentic" Jewish expression. Unlike the classical Reform experience that required a professional choir skilled in performative art music, Carlebach's music required no training, preparation, or previous knowledge. It was tailor-made for a population that was eager but untrained in traditional liturgy and Hebrew. For many younger Reform Jews, merely singing in Hebrew was a rebellion against the English texts found in the *Union Hymnal.* According to Isaacson, singing Carlebach's songs felt new and refreshing. He recalls working with Carlebach one year at Kutz, noting that he had the trappings and entourage of a star while featuring very simplified music that an audience could learn quickly.

Like Sharlin, Carlebach believed collective singing created spiritual connection. This idea rose up not only in the Jewish world but in the social movements of American folk music via Pete Seeger. Today, the influence of Carlebach's music extends beyond his specific melodies. Wordless *nigunim* are often sung now at the start of liberal worship to shape inclusivity and build a sacred moment. Carlebach essentially redefined the predominant Chasidic *nigun* as a method rather than a genre of music.

Once Carlebach's songs were part of the Israeli Chassidic Song Festival's annual offerings, his music appeared more frequently on Reform playlists. As musicologist Judah Cohen has noted, "Reform views of modern Chasidism gave Shlomo Carlebach a significant foothold from which he could create and spread a central part of his message." Certainly, his music had a major influence on the music of the Reform camps, rabbis, cantors, and music educators in the 1970s, as Jeff and Danny immersed in their studies and began their careers.

The Birth of Kol B'Seder

Danny graduated from Trinity in May of 1973 and, having decided to work for a year before starting rabbinical school in Israel, became the Hillel advisor at Wellesley College and a cantorial soloist at Temple Beth Elohim, both in Wellesley, Massachusetts. He lived in Waltham and met with Jeff frequently. Jeff, on leave from Clark University, had a part-time job as a music teacher at Temple Isaiah in Lexington and sang with the Zamir Chorale of Boston. Their proximity to each other enabled great opportunity to write music together, and that year was highly productive.

The creative process looked something like this: Jeff would take out his guitar and a tape recorder. Danny, who knew liturgy and Hebrew well, would open the prayer book and search for a passage reflecting important values. Together, they'd consider the text for musicality and review the Hebrew pronunciation to ensure proper rhythm. The tape recorder was turned on, and Jeff would play some chords or chord progressions on guitar, often ones he had absorbed from Joni Mitchell, James Taylor, or other well-known folk performers. Danny would start improvising a melody.

When something struck them as workable, they'd review it from the tape recorder, with Jeff suggesting melodic or key changes. Over time, the song would be stitched together. Then, the real test began. They would bring the piece to their next youth event to see what resonated, getting instant feedback on their compositions. The first song they wrote together was "Modeh Ani" in 1972, followed by more than a dozen, including "Shalom Rav," "Ashrei," and "V'yashvu Ish." During the summers at Eisner, where they had many opportunities to experiment with music, the two wrote "Lo Alecha," "Ushmor," "Tov L'hodot," and "Sin'u Ra." They also began working with Loui Dobin, who helped them form Kol B'Seder.

As Jeff noted about their time at camp:

> You know, if you teach a song at lunchtime and nobody likes it and it doesn't catch on, well, the song dies. But if you teach the song at lunch and people kind of react to it and start to sing it, by dinner, it's almost a hit. That's the great thing about camp. A song can be successful by the next Shabbat after they've sung it two or three times. Suddenly everybody is banging on the tables and getting up and dancing.

In March 1974, Jeff and Danny gave their first public concert at Brandeis University, where they premiered "Shalom Rav." In addition to the premiere, the concert was important because it marked the duo's reach beyond camp settings. They were now attracting Jewish college-age audiences, which they considered a step-up as a musical group. Danny remembers that particular concert for another reason: He met Elyse Frishman for the first time that evening, and the two would marry in 1978.

Camps and regional youth conferences were the laboratories in which Jeff and Danny composed and where their songs developed and changed. As they saw it, a song was never quite in its "final" form; it was always evolving with the people who sang it and performed it live. The songs they wrote during the 1970s can be heard in their original versions on the *Songs NFTY Sings* albums (now available in the box set *Complete NFTY Recordings*).

After that creative year together in Boston, Danny moved to Israel to begin rabbinical school at HUC-JIR in Jerusalem, and Jeff started cantorial school at the New York campus. When Danny returned to New York the following year to continue his studies, the Kol B'Seder band started playing *b'nei mitzvah*, weddings, and concerts for youth events and Hillel conferences. For a few years, they performed nearly every week and did more than thirty concerts a year all over New York. Danny recalls how at one event he officiated at the wedding before setting up as the singer for the band.

Between 1975 and 1987, Kol B'Seder sang at hundreds of events, including the Salute to Israel Parade in Central Park in 1978, where they performed alongside Shlomo Carlebach and Moshe Shur for Israel's thirtieth birthday celebration, and the Freedom Sunday for Soviet Jews rally in Washington, DC, in 1987. They also became regulars at the Coalition for the Advancement of Jewish Education (CAJE) conference starting in 1978, which expanded their musical reach far beyond the Reform Movement.

The first CAJE conference was held in the summer of 1976, and the annual event soon became the perfect venue for young musical groups, cantors, singers, and songwriters to showcase their work. In addition to Debbie Friedman and Kol B'Seder, in that era many other individuals and groups were creating contemporary Jewish music, including the Fabrangen Fiddlers, Beged Kefet, Julie Silver, Craig Taubman, and Doug Cotler. CAJE solidified the "contemporary Jewish music" genre, later known as "American *nusach*," and promoted cross-pollination among the movements.

Much of the music was written specifically with Hebrew schools and religious schools in mind, and ultimately educators and rabbis, such as those influenced by CAJE, brought this music into synagogues.

"Freedom Sunday" Rally for Soviet Jewry, Washington, DC, December 6, 1987. Natan Sharansky, rear left.

After Danny was ordained as a rabbi in 1979, he worked for three years as the assistant director of NFTY for the UAHC (renamed the Union for Reform Judaism in 2003) and continued his musical partnership with Jeff. In the coming decades, his career would have a dramatic influence on the development of Jewish music in the United States, far beyond the duo's reach.

Jeff was ordained as a cantor the next year, having served as a student cantor at Temple Beth El of Northern Westchester in Chappaqua, New York, during his final year of studies. He continued there for a year after ordination on a part-time basis so that he could continue to compose and perform with Danny.

At the time, most cantors still were singing the traditional Reform repertoire, so Jeff had few role models for the type of cantorate he sought to create. When an opportunity arose to spend a year in Israel as a *madrich* (counselor) to high school students on the UAHC's Eisendrath International Exchange (EIE) program then based at the Leo Baeck School in Haifa, Jeff set off for Israel. The year proved to be an exceptional experience, most notably because he was invited to compose new songs for the young, growing Reform Movement in Israel. Among the approximately twenty songs he composed during that time are three that are his personal favorites: "Oseh Shalom," "Haporeis Sukkat Shalom," and "Yeish Kochavim."

The year in Israel led him, serendipitously, to his next chapter when an EIE student from Chicago told his rabbi about Jeff. The congregation was in search of a cantor, and upon his return to the United States in 1982, Jeff moved to the Midwest to serve as cantor with Rabbi Peter Knobel at Beth Emet The Free Synagogue in Evanston, Illinois. The position was an excellent match for Jeff and the community, encouraging his vision of a new cantorate, and he had an eighteen-year tenure with the congregation.

Synagogue music was changing, as elements of folk, Chasidic, and Israeli musical styles were increasingly adapted to worship. In Chicago, Jeff was the first to accompany services with professional-level guitar playing on the bimah during worship; he was a true pioneer. Effectively and creatively, he engaged people to sing—not only listen—during services. Although not trained with an operatic vocal style, Jeff applied his voice and talents to inspire participation, and people responded. The goal was for Jews in the pews to open up their voices in worship, and the environment that Jeff was creating gave "voice," in its multiple meanings, back to the congregation. As it turned out, Jeff's location in Chicago, near a major airport hub, proved useful in keeping his work with Kol B'Seder going, despite a crazy schedule:

> I used to go to the airport on Saturday after a bar or bat mitzvah and take a 3 p.m. plane to wherever it happened to be, anywhere in the country, then do a Saturday night concert. And then Sunday morning, I would take a 6 a.m. flight home, then drive into work and teach religious school.

Meanwhile, from 1982 to 1992, Danny served as the regional director of the New Jersey–West Hudson Valley Council of the UAHC. He found this period of his career to be one of the most creative, helping to establish new congregations, create post–*b'nei mitzvah* and youth programs, and support rabbis and synagogue lay leaders. The position also was a Monday-to-Friday job with a lot of midweek evening meetings, a schedule that allowed him to travel on weekends to perform music with Jeff. In 1992, he became director of program for the UAHC in its New York office, supervising staff responsible for programming in the areas of education, campus, youth, small congregations, synagogue management, and adult outreach.

Throughout the 1980s Jeff and Danny continued to meet at events and gigs, write songs, and record albums. They also were getting to know Debbie Friedman quite well, frequently meeting her and other Jewish musicians at Reform Movement Biennials, CAJE conferences, and event concerts.

Late Twentieth-Century Shifts in Synagogue Music

In 1985, recognizing the sweep of the new sound across the country, Rabbi Alexander Schindler, president of the UAHC, called for changes in synagogue music and added a new portfolio to Danny's existing roles: director of the Commission on Synagogue Music. The Commission supported cantors, congregational singing, choirs, and laypeople invested in synagogue music with workshops, research, and publications and also encouraged a cantorial certification program for cantorial soloists.

In this new role, Danny worked with Cantor Ray Smolover and Dr. Judith Tischler, *z"l*, to create *Shaarei Shirah: Gates of Song*, published by Transcontinental Music in 1987. Although it was not a hymnal that would "live in the pews," it significantly shifted the musical repertoire of synagogues in several ways. *Shaarei Shirah* included keyboard arrangements for every melody. Because these were not intended for the organ, the primary keyboard instrument used at the time, the publication encouraged congregations to transition from organ music to piano and electric keyboard. This was especially important for smaller congregations with no organ. Additionally, worship leaders could learn the songs and then lead congregants in singing them. Overall, it uplifted the new contemporary sound.

To meet the need for more accessible music and more congregational participation, previously published compositions were edited. As part of the process, certain composed materials were presented in reduced formats and the keys were changed or lowered to accommodate congregational singing. Additionally, instead of standard, four-part choral music with individual parts for each voice, the compositions were edited to be sung by nonprofessional singers. Cantor Charles Davidson arranged the keyboard accompaniments, and Jeff provided the guitar chords for each selection.

The Commission on Synagogue Music partnered with the UAHC's Commission on Religious Living to publish a major study of synagogue music trends, *Emerging Worship and Music Trends in UAHC Congregations* (1994). Included in the study were the results of a survey that had been conducted to assess congregational practices and musical styles. The survey revealed a marked decline in organ use and a significant increase in piano, keyboard, and guitar between 1987 and 1993.

Danny remained at the UAHC, becoming its vice president in 2001 and later the URJ's senior vice president, both during Rabbi Eric Yoffie's tenure as the organization's president. In 2014, Danny became president of the World Union for Progressive Judaism, the international umbrella organization of the Reform, Liberal, Progressive, and Reconstructionist movements, until his retirement in 2019.

Conflict and Transition in Synagogue Music

As in the past, this latest change in musical worship style did not come without conflict. With historical context, it isn't surprising that new Jewish music encountered opposition in synagogues, since liturgical music throughout Western history was generally considered to be more conservative, lagging behind a society's musical trends. This truism also held for the changes in Jewish synagogue music: There was a time gap before the American Jewish community's musical taste would widely accept the new styles as "regular" synagogue worship music.

Many synagogue music directors (who were often conductors of their community's professional choirs as well) during the late twentieth century were not Jewish and played organ or keyboard. Many of these musicians were not open to the use of guitar instead of keyboard as the accompanying instrument. Learning a new repertoire and new approach to musical worship required what, for some, was a burden of time and effort. Overall, it took a generation for many congregations to shift away from an emphasis on the more formal, classical Reform styles of music.

Further, many Reform cantors and music professionals at the time opposed music that they felt was too simple to create deep religious emotion and lacked sophistication for adult worshipers; it wasn't musically "Jewish" in origin, or didn't contain *nusach*, an important feature of tradition. Some described the new songs as being "happy-clappy," a "dumbing down" of synagogue worship music, smacking of "fad," or just "going too far." Cantors had not been trained to lead group singing; their role was to inspire as a soloist with an expressive voice, accompanied by the choir and organ/keyboard, performing from an abundantly rich repertoire of through-composed music.

The conflict was not without merit. There were still substantial numbers of synagogues whose musical professionals were devoted to and invested in new, more formal compositions and believed them to provide the right ingredients for meaningful worship. And by this time there was a significant body of new, high-quality compositions by prolific modern composers, including Ben Steinberg (1930–2023) and Simon Sargon (1938–2022), that congregations around the country loved and cantors wanted to offer in their services.

While composers might have intended such compositions to be heard with professional choirs and cantors, some pieces were so well known that congregants often joined in, the familiarity creating deep communal feelings and a sense of spirituality. Steinberg's "Shalom Rav," which uses a modern idiom in an accessible style, was widely adopted.

Jack Gottlieb, another well-respected figure in Jewish music, highly admired for his compositions and teaching, felt that to diminish complexity in synagogue music would be a wrong turn. Many younger composers, including Michael Isaacson, had reservations about ascribing all worship music to camp tunes and congregational singing.

Despite these protests, many favored the new musical style. Bearing in mind that the young Jews of the camp and youth movement now were grown into adulthood and members of synagogues, many people believed that classic synagogue musical services were "spiritless" and needed more congregational participation. This new music, they contended, brought the healthy "spirit of camp" into synagogues and promoted spiritual nourishment. In addition to creating music, Jeff and Danny worked within the organized Jewish community—amid the conflict—to promote the adoption of new music.

One opportunity that they saw for informal music to enter synagogue life was new songs for religious schools. Rabbi Daniel Syme, director of education at the UAHC in the 1970s and '80s, commissioned Jeff and others to write a series of educational songs for kids. Cantor Stephen Richards was the project director and editor of the UAHC's *Manginot* (1991), a multilevel music curriculum for religious schools, which included Danny and Jeff's consultation. Much as Binder and the Goldfarbs had reintroduced traditional Jewish tunes in the overhaul to the *Union Hymnal* and the Goldfarb songbooks a half-century earlier, there was a conscious attempt to put older forms of music—more traditional Jewish tunes—together with newer music (including Kol B'Seder songs) in the *Manginot* curriculum.

As the director of the Commission on Synagogue Music and through his supervision of Transcontinental Music, Danny was uniquely positioned to affect a thoughtful and strategic musical direction to a large segment of the contemporary Jewish music world. His awareness that adults were as compelled by the new music as teens motivated the development of increased programming for adult spirituality in the 1980s and 1990s.

As a result, Jeff and Danny helped create and lead a series of Reform Movement adult study retreats called *kallot*. The music they were writing in this period was primarily directed at adults. These songs became the liturgical backbone of worship at the *kallot*, which heavily influenced the spiritual experience for those in attendance. As Jeff noted, "Our number one mission [always] has been to educate all Jewish people, not just kids." As it turned out, communal adult singing was found to be a powerful transmitter for Jewish spirituality and unity. What's more, the music was a major takeaway from the retreats; once people took it home with them, the songs became integrated into their own synagogue services.

In addition to the *kallot*, several other factors helped move Danny's and Jeff's music into the synagogue mainstream. This was the period in which those who came of age in the early years of the Reform youth movement were moving into senior leadership roles in synagogues, and they sought familiar, compelling music.

Jeff and Danny realized that by changing some of their songs' arrangements, keys, and tempos, as well as using the right keyboard arrangements, their body of work would be more universally accepted. The music of Kol B'Seder seeped into the musical repertoires of Conservative and Orthodox communities. By way of concerts, recordings, and scores, it flowed into the Jewish world and took on a life of its own, with some pieces now considered to be "authentic," composerless Jewish folk music.

As the duo's compositions became increasingly entrenched in synagogues' mainstream musical repertoires, the new songleading project Hava Nashira augmented the pace at which new Jewish music found its way into the pews. Founded in 1992 by Jeff, Debbie Friedman, and Jerry Kaye (then director at the URJ Olin-Sang-Ruby Union Camp Institute), Hava Nashira brought young camp songleaders from URJ camps to Oconomowoc, Wisconsin to hone their skills, techniques, and repertoire and be mentored by others. For the most part, these attendees were songleaders or or teachers, not cantors with formal training.

With Debbie Friedman at Hava Nashira, OSRUI, Oconomowoc, Wisconsin, June 1995

In its inaugural year, when the program was five days long, approximately fifty people attended Hava Nashira. By the early 2000s, attendance peaked at about 250. Cantor Rosalie Will joined the faculty in 1994, which early on included Jeff, Julie Silver, Craig Taubman, Danny Maseng, Merri Lovinger Arian, and Cantor Ellen Dreskin. Instruction was in the form of master classes, wherein songleaders taught a song, after which the mentors would critique their methods, offering pointers and suggestions.

In addition, Friedman, Jeff, and other songwriters would try out their new songs with the groups.Hava Nashira became known as the place to hear and learn the newest repertoire, well before the songs might be available in recorded or polished form. Often, attendees would bring these new songs home and teach them to their congregations. By the time a song was released on an album, it likely already had a following. Sometimes attendees would transcribe the songs, so variations arose. Much of the music at Hava Nashira was cross-denominational, but its home was found primarily in progressive communities.

With time, Hava Nashira evolved beyond its original mission of teaching only camp songleaders. When Friedman began writing healing music for attendees, she attracted a cadre of Jewish women who came solely for the opportunity to sing with her. Others came to become more engaging prayer leaders, to lead more social justice singing, or to offer healing through music. Hava Nashira spawned the creation of Jewish songleading professionals for camps and for congregations, where their roles extended beyond that of choir directors.

For more than thirty years, Hava Nashira has had a tremendous influence on the innovation, growth, and dissemination of new Jewish music. It has prompted important conversations about what it means to pray and how to utilize music most effectively. It has spurred and strengthened diversity in worship styles and deeper engagement of worshipers in congregations throughout North America.

Beginning in the mid-1990s and for approximately fifteen years, Danny was active on the Reform Movement's Cantorial Placement Commission. He witnessed dramatic changes to the roles of cantors. In addition to the innovation of women in the cantorate in 1975, the responsibilities of cantors shifted. Today, cantors often serve as co-clergy, rather than in a position subordinate to the rabbi, and sometimes as solo clergy. Many cantors have positions and degrees that combine multiple roles into one position, including cantor-educator and cantor-rabbi.

The Influence of Kol B'Seder

Jeff and Danny's efforts to marry original melodies with Jewish texts has had a profound and lasting impact on contemporary Jewish music. Kol B'Seder not only introduced traditional teachings to young, modern listeners but made them accessible, relatable, and memorable. Their early camp music taught Jewish heritage and values to middle and high school students, drawing texts from liturgy, *Pirkei Avot*, Mishnah, and other traditional Jewish works. This pioneering fusion of music and tradition was a powerful tool for education and engagement. By bringing the words of Jewish liturgy and texts into young people's mouths, Danny and Jeff's heartfelt and uplifting melodies also imprinted the words into their minds and hearts.

Kol B'Seder's success demonstrated the potential for innovation. Their approach inspired a new wave of creativity and experimentation among Jewish musicians who began exploring diverse musical styles and lyrical themes while remaining rooted in tradition. This ongoing evolution of Jewish music continues to enrich and enliven Jewish communities worldwide.

During the 1980s and 1990s, Kol B'Seder created songs specifically for young children through third grade to teach Jewish symbols, holiday terms, values, and Hebrew words, as well as to inculcate emotional connections to Judaism. For example, acquiring a Jewish worldview as taught through music was the goal of songs such as "This Is Very Good." The songs were designed to be easily acquired by children, and albums such as *Songs for Growin'*, first released in cassette format when cassette players were common in cars, could be readily incorporated into the lives of young families by being played during commutes, carpools, and at home.

Furthermore, Kol B'Seder's commitment to education expanded the scope of Jewish music beyond mere entertainment. Their songs became valuable resources for Jewish educators and community leaders, providing engaging and memorable ways to teach important religious and cultural concepts. Whether through catchy tunes that reinforced Hebrew vocabulary or thoughtful lyrics that explored complex theological ideas, Kol B'Seder's music played a vital role in shaping Jewish education and identity for generations of young people.

Beyond Kol B'Seder's musical and educational legacies, the songs often carried profound messages of Jewish identity, faith, and social justice in songs such as "Lo Alecha," "In Every Generation," and "V'ahavta L'rei-acha Kamocha." Over the decades, Jeff and Danny used their music as a platform to address issues facing the Jewish community, inspiring listeners to reflect on their values and beliefs, and fostering a sense of belonging, unity, solidarity, and Jewish pride.

Perhaps one of Kol B'Seder's most far-reaching and long-lasting influences on Jewish music has resulted from Danny's various roles in the Reform Movement. Beginning in the late 1970s, Danny used his positions to bring together the many creative musical strands emerging within the Movement. In 1979, he led the effort to publish NFTY's first unified songbook for its youth movement and camps, titled *Shireinu (Our Songs)*. Particularly in the 1990s and 2000s, he brought the youth movement's influence to Transcontinental Music, which the UAHC had acquired in 1975.

Transcontinental Music Publications, now owned by the American Conference of Cantors, is the oldest, largest, and today one of the few remaining publishers of Jewish music worldwide. At the dawn of the millenium, Danny and then-new TMP director Joe Eglash sought a complete revisioning of the Movement's music publishing and dissemination. This new energy brought about publications that reflected contemporary worship styles. Songbooks like *The Complete Shireinu*, now a standard book in most Jewish music libraries, and series like *Shabbat Anthology* and *Ruach* gave synagogues, clergy, music professionals, and songleaders the resources they needed to help create dynamic singing communities.

Such an impact on Jewish music went well beyond what most performers could hope to accomplish. Other than Friedman's music, which galvanized a grassroots clamor for change, the massive

CAJE 31 concert, Duke University, August 2006. Left to right: Craig Taubman, Doug Cotler, Debbie Friedman, Julie Silver, Dan, and Jeff. (Photograph by David Parker)

institutional effect Danny achieved through strategic publishing proved to be decisive in influencing the direction of sacred music for the last fifty years and long into the future.

Conclusion

The contribution of Kol B'Seder extends far beyond the realm of entertainment. Influenced by a wide range of musical styles including rock 'n' roll, folk, pop, Israeli, Chasidic, choral, and traditional Jewish music and *nusach*, its original blend created a new Jewish music: accessible, engaging, and generative. It has been a catalyst for social change and profound spiritual and communal engagement.

This anthology demonstrates the skillful melding that has made Kol B'Seder an institution in the world of Jewish music. This volume includes the music alongside analysis and commentary from Jeff and Danny, offering us a deeper understanding of the intention behind each musical composition.

These days, Danny and Jeff create less new music. They recognize with joy that the future of Jewish music is in the capable hands of a new generation of cantors and singer-songwriters.

Their greatest influence has been on the larger Jewish music scene and its scores of musicians. Their music has crossed denominational lines, becoming universal like the Yiddish and Israeli musical compositions by the Goldfarbs and Carlebach when Kol B'Seder was just starting. This crossover can be attributed not only to the music's simplicity but to its beauty, meaning, and intention as an accessible vehicle for prayer and spiritual connection.

Jeff and Danny's music is now in the mainstream of Jewish musical consciousness in America. For generations to come, their songs will continue to inspire Jewish songleaders, cantors, composers, rabbis, educators, and everyone who sings along.

– Judith S. Pinnolis
Newton, Massachusetts
Elul 5784/2024

Additional editing by Rabbi Elyse Frishman and Jane E. Herman

Selected Bibliography for *Kol B'Seder and Twentieth-Century Jewish Music*

Adelstein, Rachel. "(Shabbat) Angels in America: Israel Goldfarb, 'Shalom Aleichem,' and the Search for Nusach America." *Music and Minorities* 2 (2023): 1–27.

Benor, Sarah Bunin, Jonathan Krasner, and Sharon Avni. *Hebrew Infusion: Language and Community at American Jewish Summer Camps.* New Brunswick, NJ: Rutgers University Press, 2020.

Cohen, Judah M. "A Holy Brother's Liberal Legacy: Shlomo Carlebach, Reform Judaism, and Hasidic Pluralism." *American Jewish History* 100, no. 4 (October 2016): 485–509.

———" 'And the Youth Shall See Visions': Songleading, Summer Camps, and Identity among Reform Jewish Teenagers." In *Musical Childhoods and the Cultures of Youth*, ed. Susan Boynton and Roe-Min Kok. Middletown, CT: Wesleyan University Press, 2006.

———"Musical Tradition and the Crisis of Place: Reform Jewish Songleading, Shabbat Shirah, and the New Dining Hall." *Western Folklore* 67, no. 4 (Fall 2008): 321–49.

———" 'Sing Unto God': Debbie Friedman and the Changing Sound of Jewish Liturgical Music." *Contemporary Jewry* 35, no. 1 (April 2015): 13–34.

Edelman, Joshua. "The Debbie Friedman Problem: Performing Tradition, Memory, and Modernity in Progressive Jewish Liturgy." *Liturgy* 28, no. 1 (January 2013): 6–17.

Friedmann, Jonathan L. *Cantor William Sharlin: Musical Revolutionary of Reform Judaism.* Jefferson, NC: McFarland, 2019.

———"The Secularization of Synagogue Song: Music in American Jewish Worship." Unpublished masters thesis, California State University, 2007.

Isaacson, Michael. "Rethinking Worship Music on a Balanced Bimah." Keynote address, Hebrew Union College, Art of Synagogue Music Conference and Symposia, New York, November 12, 2006.

Kelman, Ari Y., and Shaul Magid. "The Gate to the Village." *American Jewish History* 100, no. 4 (October 2016): 511–40.

Klepper, Jeff. "Visions of Debbie Friedman." *Musica Judaica* 20 (2013–14): 263–79.

Kligman, Mark. "Contemporary Jewish Music in America." *American Jewish Year Book*, 2001, 88–141.

Leventhal, Jenna. *The Brandeis-Bardin Institute: A Living History.* Los Angeles: American Jewish University, 2012.

Lipstadt, Deborah E. " 'And It Not Be Stilled': The Legacy of Debbie Friedman." In *Between Jewish Tradition and Modernity: Rethinking an Old Opposition*, ed. Michael A. Meyers and David N. Myers. Detroit: Wayne State University Press, 2014.

Michelman, Henry. "Israel Goldfarb (1879–1967): Rabbi, Cantor and Influential Composer." *The Synagogue Journal 1856–2006*, no. 6, February 10, 2006, n.p., https://kanestreet.org/wp-content/uploads/2008/09/hjbinder06sacred_music.pdf.

Moddel, Philip. *Max Helfman: A Biographical Sketch.* Berkeley, CA: Judah L. Magnes Memorial Museum, 1974.

Ophir, Natan. "Evaluating Rabbi Shlomo Carlebach's Place in Jewish History." *American Jewish History* 100, no. 4 (October 2016): 541–46.

Reimer, Joseph. *Making Shabbat: Celebrating and Learning at American Jewish Summer Camps.* Waltham, MA: Brandeis University Press, 2022.

Rubin, Emanuel, and John H. Baron. *Music in Jewish History and Culture.* Sterling Heights, MI: Harmonie Park Press, 2006.

Sarna, Jonathan. "The Crucial Decade in Jewish Camping." In *A Place of Our Own: The Rise of Reform Jewish Camping*, ed. Michael M. Lorge and Gary P. Zola. Tuscaloosa: University of Alabama Press, 2006.

Schiller, Benjie-Ellen. "The Hymnal as an Index of Musical Change in Reform Synagogues." In *Sacred Sound and Social Change: Liturgical Music in Jewish and Christian Experience*, ed. Lawrence A. Hoffman and Janet R. Walton. Notre Dame: University of Notre Dame Press, 1992.

Clockwise from top left: Kol B'Seder Band's first performance, February 22, 1975, Temple Israel of Jamaica, New York City (Dan was in Israel!); Boston University Hillel, November 3, 1979; Zamir Chorale of Boston Tribute to Kol B'Seder concert, Cambridge, Massachusetts, June 3, 2007; Temple Shaaray Tefila, New York City, May 7, 2000.

Top: Signing autographs after a concert, date and location unknown, c. 1990. Middle: Greater Chicago Jewish Folk Arts Festival, June 22, 1986. Jeff and Dan with Peter Yarrow and Howard Levy. (Photograph by Michael M. Lorge) Bottom: URJ Biennial, Oneg Shabbat, Boston, November 6, 2015

Top left: Touring Israel (Keisarya), mid-1980s. (Photograph by Elyse Frishman) Top right: Touring Moscow during WUPJ conference, June 2005. Bottom: Zamir Chorale of Boston Tribute to Kol B'Seder concert, Sanders Theater, Cambridge, Massachusetts, June 3, 2007.

Kol B'seder Anthology

THE MUSIC OF **JEFF KLEPPER** AND **DAN FREELANDER**

Abraham

Music: **Jeff Klepper**
Text: **Jeff Klepper** and **Jeffrey Salkin**, based on Genesis 12 and 22

From the album *Bible People* (ARE) - Recorded 2024 for *Kol B'Seder Anthology*
To purchase multiple copies for your ensemble, please visit TranscontinentalMusic.com

VERSE 3
C F G
29
3. God told A - bra - ham to slay his son,___ but a voice said, "Stop!" be - fore the
C G7 C F C F C
32
deed was done. He looked in the thick - et and found a ram, and
F C D7 G
35
D.S. al Fine
God gave a bless - ing to A - bra - ham.

Adon Olam

אדון עולם

Music: **Jeff Klepper**
Text: Liturgy

From the album *Yom Chadash*
To purchase multiple copies for your ensemble, please visit TranscontinentalMusic.com

VERSES 2&4
2. V' - a - cha - rei kich - lot ha - kol,
4. V' - hu Ei - li v' - chai go - a - li, v' -
l' - va - do yim - loch no - ra. V' - hu ha - yah, v' - hu
tzur chev - li b' - eit tza - rah. V' - hu ni - si u - ma -
ho - veh, v' - hu yih' - yeh b' - tif - a - rah.
- nos li, m' - nat ko - si b' - yom ek - ra.
D.C.
Last time D.C. al Coda
CODA
VERSE 5
5. B'-ya - do af-kid ru-chi, b'-
eit i - shan v' - a - i - rah. V' - im ru - chi
g' - vi - ya - ti, A - do - nai li v' - lo i - ra.
CHORUS
La la la la la la la, la la la la la la

1. You are our Eternal God,
who reigned before any being had been created;
when all was done according to Your will,
then You were called Ruler.

1. אֲדוֹן עוֹלָם אֲשֶׁר מָלַךְ,
בְּטֶרֶם כָּל יְצִיר נִבְרָא.
לְעֵת נַעֲשָׂה בְחֶפְצוֹ כֹּל,
אֲזַי מֶלֶךְ שְׁמוֹ נִקְרָא.

2. And after all ceases to be,
You alone will rule in majesty.
You have been, are yet,
and will be in glory.

2. וְאַחֲרֵי כִּכְלוֹת הַכֹּל,
לְבַדּוֹ יִמְלוֹךְ נוֹרָא.
וְהוּא הָיָה, וְהוּא הֹוֶה,
וְהוּא יִהְיֶה, בְּתִפְאָרָה.

3. And You are One;
none other can compare to or consort with You.
You are without beginning, without end.
To You belong power and dominion.

3. וְהוּא אֶחָד וְאֵין שֵׁנִי,
לְהַמְשִׁיל לוֹ לְהַחְבִּירָה.
בְּלִי רֵאשִׁית בְּלִי תַכְלִית,
וְלוֹ הָעֹז וְהַמִּשְׂרָה.

4. And You are my God, my living Redeemer,
my Rock in times of trouble and distress.
You are my standard bearer and my refuge,
my benefactor when I call on You.

4. וְהוּא אֵלִי וְחַי גֹּאֲלִי,
וְצוּר חֶבְלִי בְּעֵת צָרָה.
וְהוּא נִסִּי וּמָנוֹס לִי,
מְנָת כּוֹסִי בְּיוֹם אֶקְרָא.

5. Into Your hands I entrust my spirit,
when I sleep and when I wake,
and with my spirit my body also;
Adonai is with me and I shall not fear.

5. בְּיָדוֹ אַפְקִיד רוּחִי,
בְּעֵת אִישַׁן וְאָעִירָה.
וְעִם רוּחִי גְּוִיָּתִי,
יְיָ לִי וְלֹא אִירָא.

Adonai, Adonai

יי יי

Music: **Jeff Klepper**
Text: Liturgy

Adonai, Adonai—God, compassionate, gracious,
endlessly patient, loving, and true;
showing mercy to the thousandth generation.

יְיָ, יְיָ, אֵל רַחוּם וְחַנּוּן,
אֶרֶךְ אַפַּיִם וְרַב־חֶסֶד וֶאֱמֶת,
נֹצֵר חֶסֶד לָאֲלָפִים.

From the album *We Are Partners*
Also available with piano accompaniment in *High Holy Days Anthology Volume II* (TMP 994060).
To purchase multiple copies for your ensemble, please visit TranscontinentalMusic.com

Adonai Oz

Y'vareich et Amo

יי עוז

יברך את-עמו

Music: **Jeff Klepper** and **Dan Freelander**
Text: Psalm 29:11

May Adonai grant strength to our people;
may Adonai bless our people with peace.

יְיָ עֹז לְעַמּוֹ יִתֵּן,
יְיָ יְבָרֵךְ אֶת־עַמּוֹ בַשָּׁלוֹם.

Af, Peh, Ozen

אף, פה, אוזן

Parts of My Body

Music and text: **Jeff Klepper**

** Have children point to the part of their body as they sing its name.*

אַף...פֶּה...אֹזֶן...עַיִן...רֶגֶל...
אַף...פֶּה...אֹזֶן...יָד...וְרֹאשׁ.

Nose, mouth, ear, eye, leg/foot,
Nose, mouth, ear, hand, and head.

שְׁתֵּי עֵינַיִם... שְׁתֵּי אׇזְנַיִם...
שְׁתֵּי יָדַיִם...אֶצְבָּעוֹת.

Two eyes, two ears,
two hands, fingers.

שְׁתֵּי עֵינַיִם... שְׁתֵּי אׇזְנַיִם...
שְׁתֵּי רַגְלַיִם...אֶצְבָּעוֹת.

Two eyes, two ears,
two feet/legs, toes.

Again and Again

Amidah for Children

Music: **Jeff Klepper**
Text: **Chaim Stern**

From the album *Songs for Growin'*
To purchase multiple copies for your ensemble, please visit TranscontinentalMusic.com

Bm7 C♯m7 D A D
God who needs our love, the God whose love we have, the God who has our
E7
love.
CHORUS
D A
A - gain and a - gain, to -
E A G D A
day and to - day, a - gain and a - gain and to - day! A -
D A E A G D
gain and a - gain, to - day and to - day, a - gain and a - gain, and to - day!
A
rit.
G D A
A - gain and a - gain, and to - day!

Ahavah Rabbah

אהבה רבה

Music: **Jeff Klepper**
Text: Morning liturgy

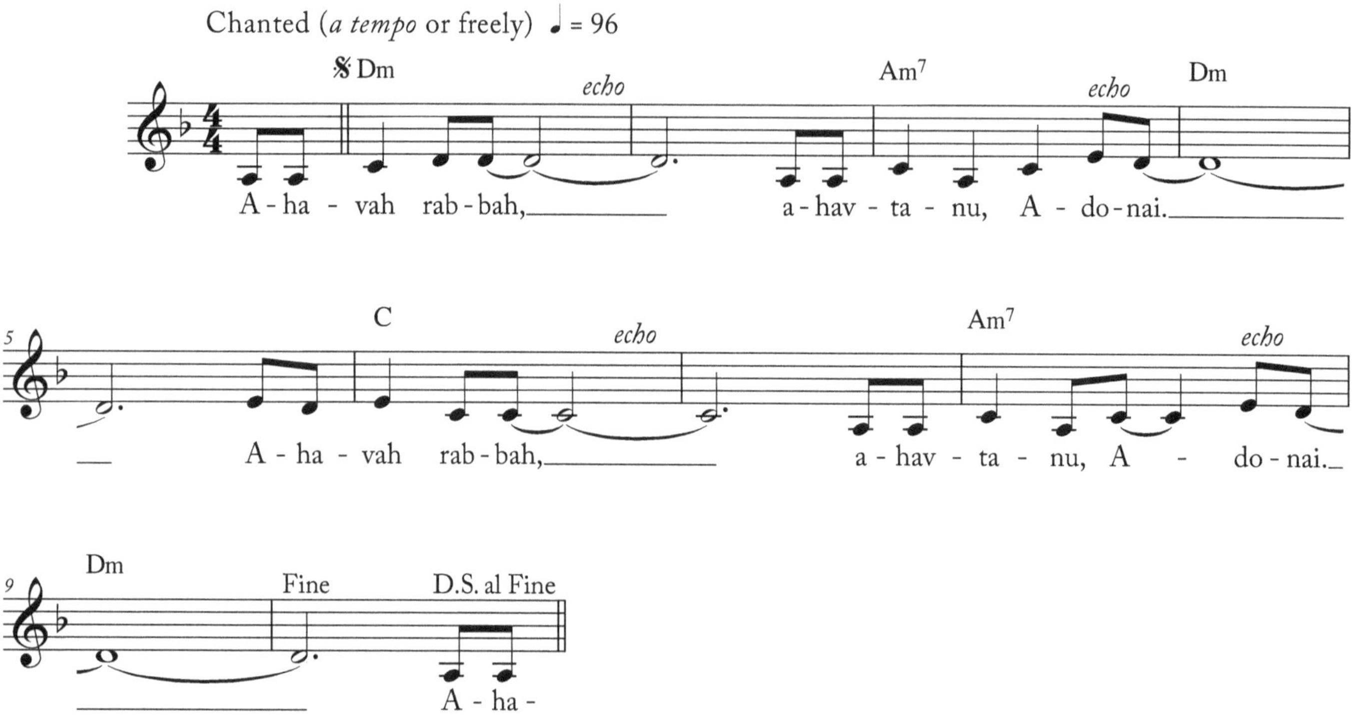

How deeply You have loved us, Adonai.

אַהֲבָה רַבָּה אֲהַבְתָּנוּ, יְיָ.

From the album *In This Place*
To purchase multiple copies for your ensemble, please visit TranscontinentalMusic.com

Al Sh'loshah D'varim I על שלושה דברים

HaOlam Omeid העולם עומד

Music: **Jeff Klepper**
Text: *Pirkei Avot* 1:2, 1:18

From the album *Sparks of Torah*

The world is sustained by three things:	עַל שְׁלֹשָׁה דְּבָרִים הָעוֹלָם עוֹמֵד:
Torah, worship,	עַל הַתּוֹרָה, וְעַל הָעֲבוֹדָה
and loving deeds.	וְעַל גְּמִילוּת חֲסָדִים.

The world is sustained by three things:	עַל שְׁלֹשָׁה דְּבָרִים הָעוֹלָם עוֹמֵד:
truth, justice,	עַל הָאֱמֶת, וְעַל הַדִּין,
and peace.	וְעַל הַשָּׁלוֹם.

Al Sh'loshah D'varim II עַל שלושה דברים

HaOlam Kayam העולם קים

Music: **Jeff Klepper**
Text: *Pirkei Avot* 1:18, ad. *Gates of Prayer*

The world is sustained by three things:
truth, justice,
and peace.

עַל שְׁלֹשָׁה דְּבָרִים הָעוֹלָם קַיָּם:
עַל הָאֱמֶת, וְעַל הַדִּין,
וְעַל הַשָּׁלוֹם.

Aleinu

עלינו

Music: **Jeff Klepper**
Text: Liturgy

Let us now praise the Sovereign of the universe,
and proclaim the greatness of the Creator
who has set us apart
from the other famlies of the earth,
giving us a destiny
unique among the nations.
We bend the knee
and bow,
acknowledging the supreme Sovereign,
the Holy One of Blessing.

עָלֵינוּ לְשַׁבֵּחַ לַאֲדוֹן הַכֹּל,
לָתֵת גְּדֻלָּה לְיוֹצֵר בְּרֵאשִׁית,
שֶׁלֹּא עָשָׂנוּ כְּגוֹיֵי הָאֲרָצוֹת,
וְלֹא שָׂמָנוּ כְּמִשְׁפְּחוֹת הָאֲדָמָה.
שֶׁלֹּא שָׂם חֶלְקֵנוּ כָּהֶם,
וְגֹרָלֵנוּ כְּכָל־הֲמוֹנָם.
וַאֲנַחְנוּ כּוֹרְעִים
וּמִשְׁתַּחֲוִים וּמוֹדִים,
לִפְנֵי מֶלֶךְ מַלְכֵי הַמְּלָכִים
הַקָּדוֹשׁ בָּרוּךְ הוּא.

From the album *We Are Partners*
Also available with piano accompaniment in *Jeff Klepper Anthology* (TMP 993117).
To purchase multiple copies for your ensemble, please visit TranscontinentalMusic.com

Anah Halach Dodeich אנה הלך דודך

Music: **Jeff Klepper**
Hebrew text: Song of Songs 6:1-2

Where has your beloved gone, fairest of women?
Where has your beloved turned? Let us seek him with you.
My beloved has gone down to his garden, to the beds of spices,
to browse in the gardens and to pick lilies.

אָנָה הָלַךְ דּוֹדֵךְ הַיָּפָה בַּנָּשִׁים
אָנָה פָּנָה דוֹדֵךְ וּנְבַקְשֶׁנּוּ עִמָּךְ.
דּוֹדִי יָרַד לְגַנּוֹ לַעֲרוּגוֹת הַבֹּשֶׂם
לִרְעוֹת בַּגַּנִּים וְלִלְקֹט שׁוֹשַׁנִּים.

From the album *Yom Chadash*

Another Year, Another Chanukah

Music and text: **Jeff Klepper** and **Dan Freelander**

From the album *In Every Generation*
To purchase multiple copies for your ensemble, please visit TranscontinentalMusic.com

Em Gm A7 C7 CHORUS G B♭
- dle glow. Be-cause it's Cha-nu-kah, ga-ther 'round the
D F G B♭
can - dle light. An-oth-er year, an-oth-er Cha - nu - kah,
Em Gm C E♭ A C
keep the dream of free-dom in your sight. Wish your friends a hap-py
G B♭ D F
Cha-nu-kah, shin-ing lights to keep us strong. An-oth-er year, an-oth-er
G B♭ last time rit. C E♭ D F Fine
Cha - nu - kah, light a can - dle, come and sing a - long.
VERSE 3 G B♭ D F
3. We strug-gle and won - der if free-dom will win. We fight a-gainst dark-
G B♭ D F G B♭
- ness for light to come in. With voic - es to - ge - ther we kin - dle these

Bm Dm
G B♭ N.C.
Bm Dm
lights on a cold, win - ter night. But the
G B♭
D F
A C
D F
G B♭
D F
days are short and we have on - ly be - gun to bring the light of free - dom to
Em Gm
A C
D.S. al Fine
ev - ery - one. And now it's

Ashrei אשרי

Music: **Jeff Klepper** and **Dan Freelander**
Text: Psalms 84:5, 144:15 (Morning liturgy)

Happy are those who dwell in Your house;
they forever praise You!
Happy the people who have it so;
happy the people whose God is Adonai.

אַשְׁרֵי יוֹשְׁבֵי בֵיתֶךָ,
עוֹד יְהַלְלוּךָ סֶּלָה.
אַשְׁרֵי הָעָם שֶׁכָּכָה לּוֹ,
אַשְׁרֵי הָעָם שֶׁיְיָ אֱלֹהָיו.

Originally from the album *Songs NFTY Sings* – Alternate version on the Kol B'Seder album *Kol B'Seder in Concert*
To purchase multiple copies for your ensemble, please visit TranscontinentalMusic.com

Ashrei Adam Matza Chochmah

אשרי אדם מצא חכמה

Music and English text: **Jeff Klepper** and **Dan Freelander**
Hebrew text: Proverbs 3:13-14

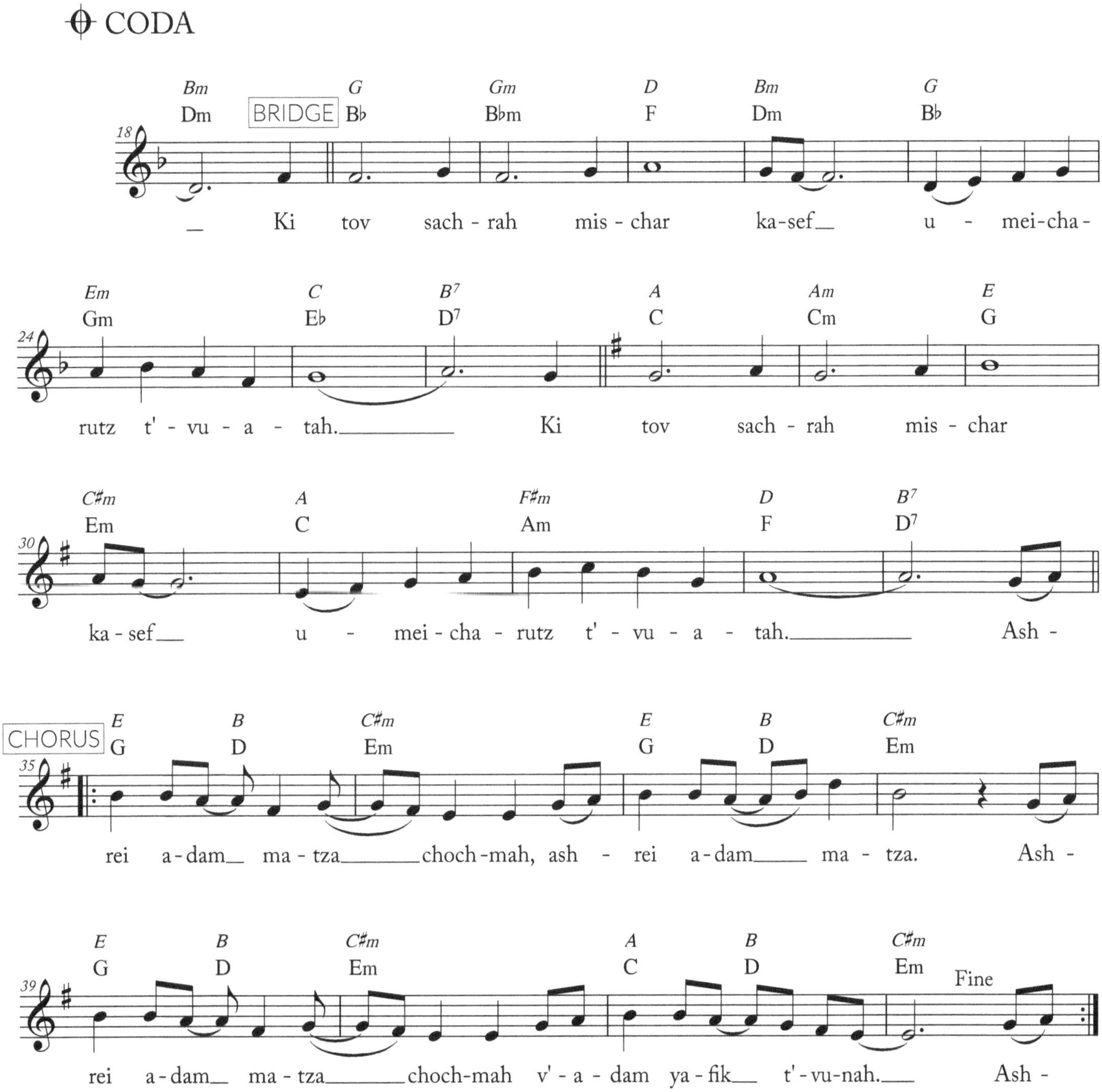

Happy is the person who finds wisdom,
the person who attains understanding.
Its value in trade is better than silver,
its yield greater than gold.

אַשְׁרֵי אָדָם מָצָא חָכְמָה
וְאָדָם יָפִיק תְּבוּנָה.
כִּי טוֹב סַחְרָהּ מִסְּחַר־כָּסֶף
וּמֵחָרוּץ תְּבוּאָתָהּ.

Ashreinu אשרינו

Music: **Jeff Klepper**
Text: Liturgy

How blessed we are: how goodly is our portion,
how delightful our lot,
how beautiful our inheritance!

אַשְׁרֵינוּ, מַה טּוֹב חֶלְקֵנוּ,
וּמַה נָּעִים גּוֹרָלֵנוּ,
וּמַה יָּפָה יְרֻשָּׁתֵנוּ.

From the album *Sparks of Torah*
Also available with piano accompaniment in *Gates of Song* (TMP 992000).
To purchase multiple copies for your ensemble, please visit TranscontinentalMusic.com

Avinu Malkeinu אבינו מלכנו

Music: **Jeff Klepper**
Text: High Holy Day liturgy

optional segue into traditional "Avinu Malkeinu" in E

Avinu Malkeinu—Almighty and Merciful—
answer us with grace, for our deeds are wanting.
Save us through acts of justice
and love.

אָבִינוּ מַלְכֵּנוּ, חָנֵּנוּ וַעֲנֵנוּ,
כִּי אֵין בָּנוּ מַעֲשִׂים.
עֲשֵׂה עִמָּנוּ צְדָקָה וָחֶסֶד,
וְהוֹשִׁיעֵנוּ.

From the album *We Are Partners*

Baruch She-amar

ברוך שאמר

Music: **Jeff Klepper**
Text: Morning liturgy

From the album *We Are Partners*
To purchase multiple copies for your ensemble, please visit TranscontinentalMusic.com

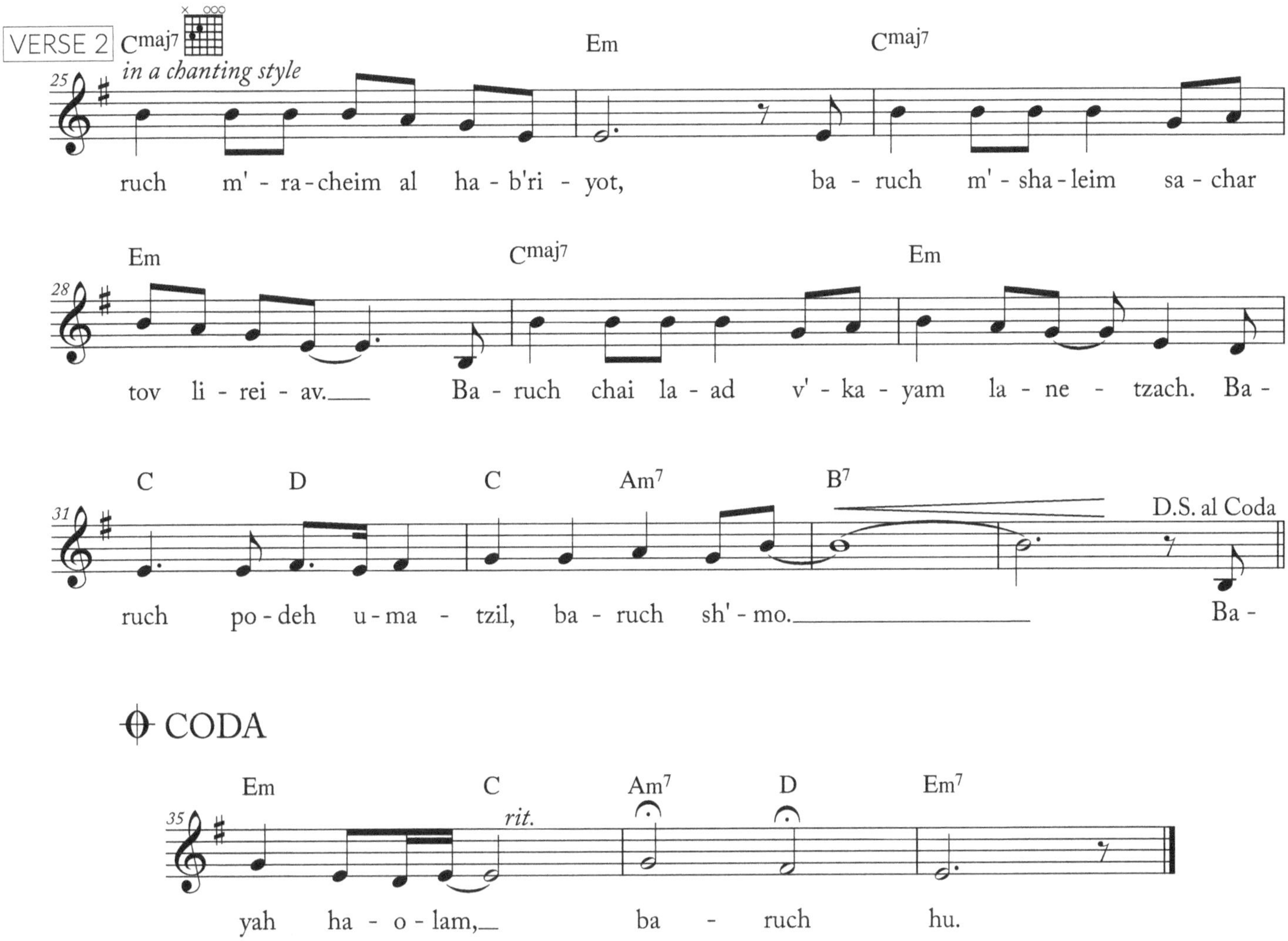

Blessed is the One who spoke and the world came to be.
Blessed is the One!
Blessed is the One who continually authors creation.
Blessed is the One whose word is deed;
blessed is the One who decrees and fulfills.
Blessed is the One who is compassionate toward the world;
blessed is the One who is compassionate toward all creatures.
Blessed is the One who rewards the reverent;
blessed is the One who exists for all time, ever-enduring.
Blessed is the One who redeems and saves; blessed is God's name!

בָּרוּךְ שֶׁאָמַר וְהָיָה הָעוֹלָם,
בָּרוּךְ הוּא.
בָּרוּךְ עֹשֶׂה בְרֵאשִׁית,
בָּרוּךְ אוֹמֵר וְעוֹשֶׂה,
בָּרוּךְ גּוֹזֵר וּמְקַיֵּם,
בָּרוּךְ מְרַחֵם עַל הָאָרֶץ,
בָּרוּךְ מְרַחֵם עַל הַבְּרִיּוֹת,
בָּרוּךְ מְשַׁלֵּם שָׂכָר טוֹב לִירֵאָיו.
בָּרוּךְ חַי לָעַד וְקַיָּם לָנֶצַח.
בָּרוּךְ פּוֹדֶה וּמַצִּיל, בָּרוּךְ שְׁמוֹ.

Bayom Hahu ביום ההוא

Music: **Jeff Klepper**
Text: Liturgy

Thus it has been said, Adonai
will be Sovereign over all the earth.
On that day, Adonai will be one,
and God's name will be one.

וְנֶאֱמַר, וְהָיָה יְיָ
לְמֶלֶךְ עַל כָּל הָאָרֶץ.
בַּיּוֹם הַהוּא יִהְיֶה יְיָ אֶחָד
וּשְׁמוֹ אֶחָד.

From the album *Yom Chadash*
Also available with piano accompaniment in *Jeff Klepper Anthology* (TMP 993117).
To purchase multiple copies for your ensemble, please visit TranscontinentalMusic.com

The Bimah Song

Music: **Jeff Klepper**
Text: **Jeff Klepper** and **Susan Nanus**

VERSE 2
D G Em C A
when you read the To-rah or take part in the ser-vice, you should-n't feel___ nerv-ous; there's
D A D G Em
not a thing to fear. So when the rab - bi calls you, ap - proach the *bi - mah* proud-ly and
C A D A D7 D.S. al Coda
read your por - tion loud - ly so ev - ery one can hear!
CODA
D A D G Em
sit-ting in my chair! I'd like to be on the *bi- mah* and lead us all in prayer. I'd
C A D G A D G D
rath - er be on the *bi - mah* than sit - ting in my chair!

B'sefer Chayim בספר חיים

Music: **Jeff Klepper**
Text: High Holy Day liturgy

From the album *We Are Partners*
Also available with piano accompaniment in *High Holy Days Anthology Volume I* (TMP 994043).
To purchase multiple copies for your ensemble, please visit TranscontinentalMusic.com

בְּסֵֽפֶר חַיִּים,
בְּרָכָה וְשָׁלוֹם וּפַרְנָסָה טוֹבָה,
נִזָּכֵר וְנִכָּתֵב לְפָנֶֽיךָ,
אֲנַֽחְנוּ וְכָל עַמְּךָ בֵּית יִשְׂרָאֵל,
לְחַיִּים טוֹבִים וּלְשָׁלוֹם.
בָּרוּךְ אַתָּה, יְיָ, עוֹשֵׂה הַשָּׁלוֹם.

In the Book of Life,
blessing, peace, and prosperity,
may we be remembered and inscribed by You,
we and all Your people Israel
for a good life and for peace.
Blessed are You, Adonai, who makes peace.

Chanukah Lights

Music and text: **Jeff Klepper** and **Dan Freelander**

From the album *Songs for Growin'*

Chatzi Kaddish

חצי קדיש

Music: **Jeff Klepper**
Text: Liturgy

Light rock ♩ = 116
For solo and congregation / choir responses (in parentheses)

From the album *We Are Partners*
Also available with piano accompaniment in *Jeff Klepper Anthology* (TMP 993117).
To purchase multiple copies for your ensemble, please visit TranscontinentalMusic.com

Exalted and hallowed be God's great name,	יִתְגַּדַּל וְיִתְקַדַּשׁ שְׁמֵהּ רַבָּא,
in the world which God created, according to plan.	בְּעָלְמָא דִּי בְרָא כִרְעוּתֵהּ.
May God's majesty be revealed	וְיַמְלִיךְ מַלְכוּתֵהּ
in the days of our lifetime	בְּחַיֵּיכוֹן וּבְיוֹמֵיכוֹן
and the life of all Israel—	וּבְחַיֵּי דְכָל בֵּית יִשְׂרָאֵל,
speedily, imminently.	בַּעֲגָלָא וּבִזְמַן קָרִיב,
To which we say: Amen.	וְאִמְרוּ: אָמֵן.
Blessed be God's great name	יְהֵא שְׁמֵהּ רַבָּא מְבָרַךְ
to all eternity.	לְעָלַם וּלְעָלְמֵי עָלְמַיָּא.
Blessed, praised, honored,	יִתְבָּרַךְ וְיִשְׁתַּבַּח וְיִתְפָּאַר
exalted, extolled,	וְיִתְרוֹמַם וְיִתְנַשֵּׂא
glorified, adored, and lauded	וְיִתְהַדָּר וְיִתְעַלֶּה וְיִתְהַלָּל
be the name of the Holy Blessed One,	שְׁמֵהּ דְּקֻדְשָׁא בְּרִיךְ הוּא,
beyond all earthly words and songs	לְעֵלָּא מִן כָּל בִּרְכָתָא וְשִׁירָתָא,
of blessing, praise, and comfort.	תֻּשְׁבְּחָתָא וְנֶחֱמָתָא,
To which we say: Amen.	דַּאֲמִירָן בְּעָלְמָא, וְאִמְרוּ: אָמֵן.

Chazak, Chazak

חזק חזק

Music: **Jeff Klepper**
Text: Based on II Samuel 10:12
Recited at the completion of each book of Torah

Chant ♩ = 112-116
May be performed as a song (with optional chords) or as a meditative chant

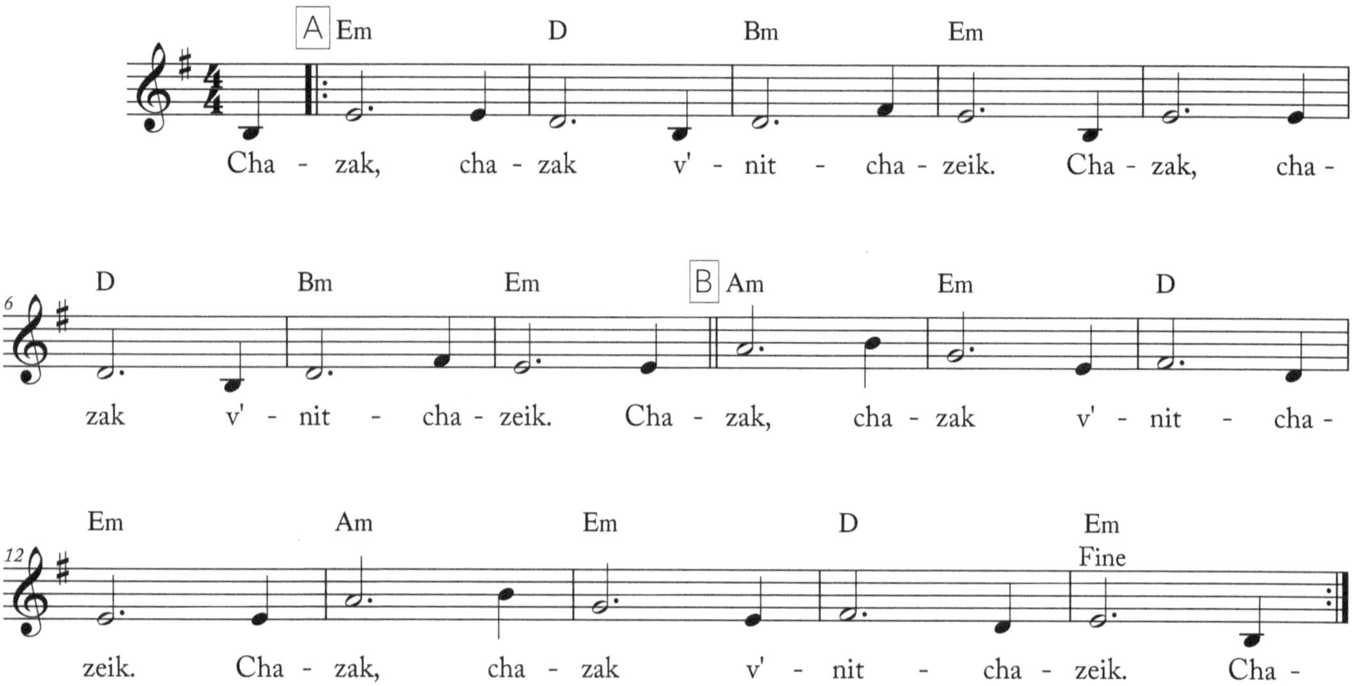

From strength to strength, and let us be strengthened.

חֲזַק חֲזַק וְנִתְחַזֵּק.

From the album *We Are Partners*
To purchase multiple copies for your ensemble, please visit TranscontinentalMusic.com

994055

Coming Home

Music and text: **Jeff Klepper**

D Am C G
cause we stood to-geth-er they'll no long-er be a-lone.__ Com-ing
Em E♭ A7 D.S. VERSE 2 Bm
home, l'-sha-lom, com-ing home. Com-ing (2.) cit-y deep in Rus-sia a re-
D E♭ Bm
fus-nik now is free. The years of wait-ing o-ver, she re-joins her fam-i-ly.__ If we
D Am C G
stand as one, to-geth-er, they will nev-er be a-lone.__ Com-ing
Em E♭ A7 D.S. VERSE 3 Bm
home, l'-sha-lom, com-ing home. Com-ing (3.)__ we have re-turned, but our
D E♭
task is not com-plete.__ There are ques-tions we must an-swer, there are
Bm D Am C
chal-len-ges to meet._ But if we learn to live to-geth-er we can build a peace-ful
G a tempo Em E♭ A7 D.S. al Coda
home. Com-ing home, l'-sha-lom, com-ing home. Com-ing

CODA

34
A G D G
home. Com-ing home, l' - sha - lom, com-ing home, l' - sha -
38
D G D
rit.
lom, com-ing home, l' - sha - lom.

Cowboy Jew from Mars

Music and text: **Jeff Klepper**

Before teaching the song, you may ask children questions about Jewish foods, rituals, and other vocabulary not usually found in children's music (e.g., supernova, petri dish). "Who likes gefilte fish?" "What does daven *mean?" After teaching the song, try replacing the word "challah" (in the chorus) with another Jewish food such as "matzah," "kugel" or "bagel."*

994055

VERSE 2
E Am G C
(2.) thing we serve is ko - sher, we grow it in a pe - tri dish. I built a
E Am D7 G G/F G/E G/D D.S.
spe-cial pool and filled it with a school of de - li-cious ge - fil - te fish! I'm a
VERSE 3
E Am G C
(3.) Jew - ish con - stel - la - tion you may have nev - er seen. And when the
E Am D7 accel.
night is clear, you'll see a ba - gel and a shmear, with a su - per - no - va in be -
G G/F G/E G/D D.S. al Coda
tween! I'm a
CODA
G7 C F
ride a-round the plan-ets and stars. I'm a Cow-boy Jew from Mars, I eat
G7 C F
cha-lah and can - dy bars, I'm a Jew-ish Mar - tian so I can't stop nosh-in' as I
G7 accel. C
ride a-round the plan- ets, ride a-round the plan- ets, ride a-round the plan - ets and stars.

Eichah Ashir איכה אשיר

Music: **Jeff Klepper** and **Dan Freelander**
Text: **Yosef Zvi Rimon**

How can I sing of day and night,
when it is God who formed them?

אֵיכָה אָשִׁיר עַל־יוֹם וָלָיְלָה—
וֵאלֹהִים הוּא יְצָרָם!

How can I sing of heaven and earth,
when it is God who decreed them?

אֵיכָה אָשִׁיר עַל־שָׁמַיִם וָאָרֶץ—
וֵאלֹהִים הוּא יְסָדָם!

How can I sing of mountains and hills,
when it is God who planted them?

אֵיכָה אָשִׁיר עַל־הָרִים וּגְבָעוֹת—
וֵאלֹהִים הוּא טְבָעָם!

How can I sing of seas and deserts,
when it is God who begot them?

אֵיכָה אָשִׁיר עַל־יַמִּים וְצִיּוֹת—
וֵאלֹהִים הוּא חוֹלְלָם!

And how can I sing of earth and its fullness,
when it is God who bade them be?

אֵיכָה אָשִׁיר עַל־תֵּבֵל וּמְלוֹאָהּ—
וֵאלֹהִים הוּא צִוָּה!

I shall sing to God who fashioned all and is beyond all—
it is to God I shall sing!

אָשִׁיר לְיוֹצֵר הַכֹּל וְנַעֲלֶה עַל־כֹּל—
לֵאלֹהִים אָשִׁירָה!

Eilu D'varim

אלו דברים

Music: **Jeff Klepper**
Text: Morning liturgy

To end the song, the bridge and final chorus may be sung together

From the album *Sparks of Torah*

Am Em C B7 Am Em
hach-na-sat ka-lah, ul-va-yat ha-meit, v'-i-yun t'fi-lah,
D Em A C Am
v'-i-yun t'fi-lah, va-ha-va-at sha-lom bein a-dam la-cha-vei-
BRIDGE
F♯m B7 continue Em C Am D Em C
ro, v'-tal-mud To-rah k'-ne-ged ku-lam, v'-tal-mud To-rah
Am D Em C Am
k'-ne-ged ku-lam. V'-tal-mud To-rah k'-ne-ged ku-
CHORUS
C D Em B7 Em C D Em
lam. Ei-lu d'-va-rim she-ein la-hem shi-ur,
C D Em C
ei-lu d'-va-rim she-ein la-hem shi-ur, ei-lu d'-va-rim she-ein la-
Am C D Em
hem shi-ur, v'-ei-lu hein.

These are things that are limitless.
They are:
honoring one's father and mother,
engaging in deeds of compassion,
arriving early for study,
morning and evening,
dealing graciously with guests,
visiting the sick,
providing for the wedding couple,
accompanying the dead for burial,
being devoted in prayer,
and making peace
among people.
But the study of Torah encompasses them all.

אֵלּוּ דְבָרִים שֶׁאֵין לָהֶם שִׁעוּר.
וְאֵלּוּ הֵן:
כִּבּוּד אָב וָאֵם,
וּגְמִילוּת חֲסָדִים,
וְהַשְׁכָּמַת בֵּית הַמִּדְרָשׁ
שַׁחֲרִית וְעַרְבִית,
וְהַכְנָסַת אוֹרְחִים,
וּבִקּוּר חוֹלִים,
וְהַכְנָסַת כַּלָּה,
וּלְוָיַת הַמֵּת,
וְעִיּוּן תְּפִלָּה,
וַהֲבָאַת שָׁלוֹם
בֵּין אָדָם לַחֲבֵרוֹ.
וְתַלְמוּד תּוֹרָה כְּנֶגֶד כֻּלָּם.

Elohim Y'choneinu אלוהים יחננו

Psalm 67

Music: **Jeff Klepper**
Text: Psalm 67:2

The A section may be sung as a round, beginning every two or four bars, or as an echo delayed by one beat

May God be gracious to us and bless us.
May God show us favor, *selah*.

אֱלֹהִים יְחָנֵּנוּ וִיבָרְכֵנוּ.
יָאֵר פָּנָיו אִתָּנוּ סֶלָה.

Empty Chair

Music and text: **Jeff Klepper**

From the album *In This Place* – Alternate version on *Jeff Klepper Live In Concert*
To purchase multiple copies for your ensemble, please visit TranscontinentalMusic.com

27
Em C Am7
we sing this song to you, Ei - li - ya - hu
31
D Em
ha - na - vi.
To Verses
Last time to Coda
VERSE 2
B7 Em C
33
2. At the se-der is an emp-ty cup, we take our wine and fill it up.
Am Bm Em
37
Then the chil-dren o-pen up the door, tell us all who we've been wait-ing for.
B7 Em C
41
Shab-bat is o-ver and we call your name, wine and spi - ces and a twist-ed flame.
Am B7 Em
45
Ei - li - ya - hu, may there come a day when no long - er will we have to say:
D.S.
VERSE 3
B7 Em C
49
3. Did you ev - er take an emp-ty space and turn it in - to a sa-cred place?
Am Bm Em
53
You can make it hap-pen an - y - where that's the mean-ing of an emp-ty chair.

57
C Em C Em C
There is an emp - ty chair,
but no one's sit - ting there.
63
Am Bm Em
D.S. al Coda
There's a feel - ing in the air,
but noth-ing in the emp-ty chair.
CODA
67
C D Em
rit.
Ei - li - ya - hu
ha - na - vi.

Esa Einai

אשא עיני

Music: **Jeff Klepper**
Text: Psalm 121:1-2

I lift my eyes to the mountains; from where does my help come?
My help comes from God, maker of heaven and earth.

אֶשָּׂא עֵינַי אֶל־הֶהָרִים, מֵאַיִן יָבֹא עֶזְרִי?
עֶזְרִי מֵעִם יְיָ, עֹשֵׂה שָׁמַיִם וָאָרֶץ.

From the album *In This Place*

Give Me Sleep

השכיבנו

Hashkiveinu

Music: **Jeff Klepper**
Text: **Chaim Stern**

35
Em F C D(sus4) D
an - gels' wings, and with their mu - sic ease our hearts.
E
40
D/A G C G D Em
Cov - er us with Your mer - cy, cov - er us with Your care,
44
D G C Em Am D
with Your bless - ing cov - er us, cov - er us, cov - er us.
F
50
Fmaj7 Cmaj7 Fmaj7 Gmaj7
optional instrumental
G
58
C G C G
Praise, praise to You, for the mel - o - dy of Your wings, as they
62
Em C Em7 A
cov - er us with peace, as they cov - er us with peace, as they
66
C C/B Am7 D G G(sus4) G
cov - er us with peace.
71
Em Em7 F C G(sus4) G
rit.

Halomeid הלומד

Music: **Jeff Klepper**
Text: *Pirkei Avot* 6:3

From the album *In Every Generation*
To purchase multiple copies for your ensemble, please visit TranscontinentalMusic.com

 994055

If we learn from others one chapter,	הַלּוֹמֵד מֵחֲבֵרוֹ פֶּרֶק אֶחָד,
or one *halachah* [Jewish law],	אוֹ הֲלָכָה אֶחָת,
one verse,	אוֹ פָּסוּק אֶחָד,
one saying,	אוֹ דִבּוּר אֶחָד,
or even one letter,	אוֹ אֲפִילוּ אוֹת אֶחָת,
we are obliged to show honor to them.	צָרִיךְ לִנְהָג בּוֹ כָּבוֹד.

Haneirot Halalu הנרות הללו

Music: **Jeff Klepper**
Text: Chanukah liturgy / Israeli Reform siddur

We kindle these lights for the miracles,	הַנֵּרוֹת הַלָּלוּ אֲנַחְנוּ מַדְלִיקִים
the wonders, the deliverances,	עַל הַנִּסִּים, וְעַל הַנִּפְלָאוֹת
and the wars (comfort) that You brought	וְעַל הַתְּשׁוּעוֹת וְעַל הַמִּלְחָמוֹת (הַנֶּחָמוֹת),
for our ancestors	שֶׁעָשִׂיתָ לַאֲבוֹתֵינוּ, שֶׁעָשִׂיתָ לְאִמּוֹתֵינוּ,
in those days at this time of year.	בַּיָּמִים הָהֵם בַּזְּמַן הַזֶּה.

From the album *Yom Chadash*

Hanitzanim

הנצנים

Music: **Jeff Klepper**
Text: Song of Songs 2:11-12

Originally from the album *Yom Chadash* – From the Kol B'Seder album *The Bridge*

The blossoms have appeared in the land,	הַנִּצָּנִים נִרְאוּ בָאָרֶץ,
the time of pruning has come.	עֵת הַזָּמִיר הִגִּיעַ.
For now the winter is past,	כִּי־הִנֵּה הַסְּתָו עָבָר,
the rains are over and gone.	הַגֶּשֶׁם חָלַף הָלַךְ לוֹ.
The song of the turtledove is heard in our land.	וְקוֹל הַתּוֹר נִשְׁמַע בְּאַרְצֵנוּ.

Haporeis Sukkat Shalom

הפורש סוכת שלום

Music: **Jeff Klepper**
Text: Evening liturgy

Blessed are You, Adonai,
Guardian of Israel, whose shelter of peace is spread over us,
over all Your people Israel, and over Jerusalem.

בָּרוּךְ אַתָּה, יְיָ,
הַפּוֹרֵשׂ סֻכַּת שָׁלוֹם עָלֵינוּ
וְעַל כָּל עַמּוֹ יִשְׂרָאֵל וְעַל יְרוּשָׁלָיִם.

Originally from the album *Yom Chadash*. From the Kol B'Seder album *Sparks of Torah*
Also available with piano accompaniment in *Jeff Klepper Anthology* (TMP 993117).
To purchase multiple copies for your ensemble, please visit TranscontinentalMusic.com

Hashiveinu

השיבנו

Music: **Jeff Klepper**
Text: Lamentations 5:21

From the album *Sparks of Torah*
Also available with piano accompaniment in *Shirei T'shuvah: Songs of Repentance* (TMP 991900).
To purchase multiple copies for your ensemble, please visit TranscontinentalMusic.com

CODA

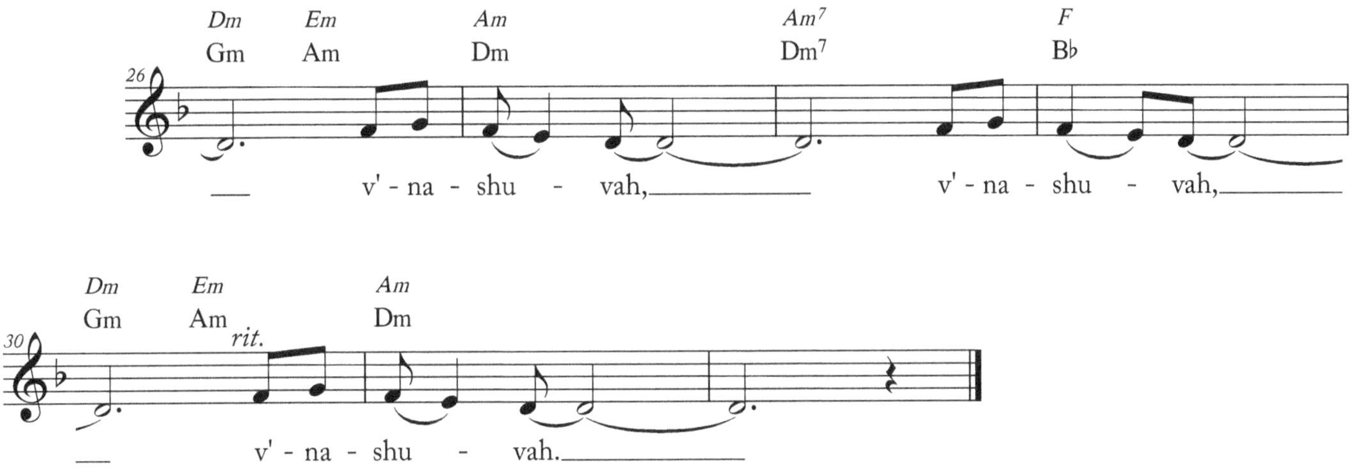

Return us to You and we will return.
Renew our days as of old!

הֲשִׁיבֵנוּ, יְיָ, אֵלֶיךָ וְנָשׁוּבָה;
חַדֵּשׁ יָמֵינוּ כְּקֶדֶם.

Healing Prayer

Adonai Y'vareich

יי יברך

Music and English text: **Jeff Klepper**
Hebrew text: Adapted from Mordechai Kaplan

From the album *We Are Partners*
To purchase multiple copies for your ensemble, please visit TranscontinentalMusic.com

Adonai will bless and heal the afflicted,	יְיָ יְבָרֵךְ וִירַפֵּא אֶת הַחוֹלִים,
All the afflicted of Israel.	כָּל הַחוֹלֵי יִשְׂרָאֵל,
And will send a speedy, complete healing,	וְיִשְׁלַח מְהֵרָה רְפוּאָה שְׁלֵמָה,
Healing of the soul and healing of the body.	רְפוּאַת הַנֶּפֶשׁ, וּרְפוּאַת הַגּוּף.
God will add for them years of life.	יְיָ, יוֹסִיף לָהֶם שְׁנוֹת חַיִּים.
To give thanks and praise to the faithful Healer	לְהוֹדוֹת וּלְהַלֵּל לָרוֹפֵא הַנֶּאֱמָן
For length of days. And we say: amen.	לְאֹרֶךְ יָמִים. וְנֹאמַר: אָמֵן.

English translation by Jeff Klepper

Hineih Mah Tov Blues הנה מה-טוב

Music: **Jeff Klepper**
Text: Psalm 133:1

From the album *Jeff Klepper Live in Concert*
To purchase multiple copies for your ensemble, please visit TranscontinentalMusic.com

𝄌 CODA

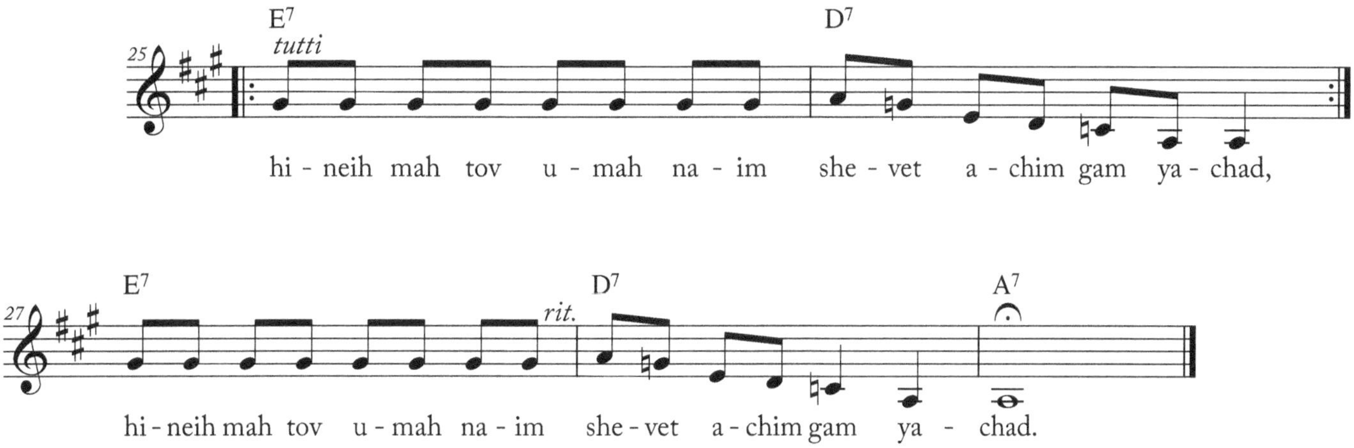

How good and how pleasant it is
that brothers / sisters dwell together.

הִנֵּה מַה־טּוֹב וּמַה־נָּעִים
שֶׁבֶת אַחִים גַּם־יָחַד.

Hodo al Eretz הודו על ארץ

Music: **Jeff Klepper** and **Dan Freelander**
Text: Psalm 148:13-14

God's majesty is above the earth and heaven;	הודו עַל אֶרֶץ וְשָׁמָיִם.
and God is the strength of our people,	וַיָּרֶם קֶרֶן לְעַמּוֹ,
making God's faithful ones,	תְּהִלָּה לְכָל־חֲסִידָיו,
Israel, a people close to the Eternal.	לִבְנֵי יִשְׂרָאֵל עַם־קְרֹבוֹ.
Halleluyah!	הַלְלוּ־יָהּ!

Hold Fast to Dreams

The Bridge

Music: **Jeff Klepper**
Text: **Yehoash** ("The Bridge") and **Langston Hughes** ("Hold Fast to Dreams")

Originally from the album *Songs NFTY Sings* – From the Kol B'Seder album *The Bridge*

G C D C Em
weight to bear,__ give me strength their weight to__ bear.__
Am D D G C G
Hold fast to dreams, for if dreams die,__
C Em C Am
__ life is a bro - ken winged bird__ that can - not fly.__
D7 G C G
Hold fast to dreams, for when dreams go,__
C Em F C
__ life is a bar - ren field__ fro - zen__ with snow.__
Am D7 G C G
Hold fast to dreams, hold fast to dreams,__
C G rit. C D7 G
hold fast to dreams,__ hold fast to dreams.

I Will Plant for My Children

Honi's Song

Music and text: **Jeff Klepper**

From the album *We Are Partners*
To purchase multiple copies for your ensemble, please visit TranscontinentalMusic.com

G Bb C Eb F Ab
21
point-ed to the trees reach-ing up to the skies. "When I came in - to this world_ there was
C Eb G Bb Em Gm Am Cm
24
fruit here for me be-cause my an - ces - tors plant-ed those trees." So I will
𝄋 B
F Ab C Eb F Ab C Eb
27
plant for my daugh-ters, I will plant for my sons, and if you ask me
G Bb Am Cm G Bb C Eb F Ab G Bb C Eb F Ab
30
why: As my par-ents plant - ed for me, I will plant for the
G Bb Em7 Gm7 Am Cm
34
ones yet to be.
Fine
C
Am Cm
Ho - ni looked at life from a
C Eb Dm Fm Am Cm
38
cir - cle of love. He prayed from his heart for rain from a - bove. He
C Eb Dm Fm
41
thought a - bout that man as the sea - sons turned, and the les - son he had
Am Cm
D.S. al Fine
44
learned. I will

Ilu Finu

אלו פינו

Music and English text: **Jeff Klepper**
Hebrew text: Morning liturgy

Even if our mouths were full of song as the sea,
we could never thank You adequately, Adonai.

אִלּוּ פִינוּ מָלֵא שִׁירָה כַּיָּם.
אֵין אֲנַחְנוּ מַסְפִּיקִים לְהוֹדוֹת לְךָ.

Im Ein Ani Li אם אין אני לי

Music: **Jeff Klepper** and **Dan Freelander**
Text: *Pirkei Avot* 1:14

From the album *In Every Generation*
To purchase multiple copies for your ensemble, please visit TranscontinentalMusic.com

If I am not for myself, who will be for me?
And if I am only for myself, what am I?
And if not now, when?

אִם אֵין אֲנִי לִי, מִי לִי?
וּכְשֶׁאֲנִי לְעַצְמִי, מָה אֲנִי?
וְאִם לֹא עַכְשָׁיו, אֵימָתַי?

I'm Growin'

Music and text: **Jeff Klepper**

Originally from the album *To See the World Through Jewish Eyes Vol. 2* (UAHC) – From the Kol B'Seder album *Songs for Growin'*
To purchase multiple copies for your ensemble, please visit TranscontinentalMusic.com

VERSE 2
G D D7
2. Grow - in' up in the world__ to-day you can lose your i-den-ti - ty,__ so the
G Em E7 A7 D.S. al Coda
way to keep on grow - in'__ is to do things Jew-ish - ly!__ I'm
CODA
E A7 E A7
__ means a lot, that__ means a lot, that__
E A7 D G D
__ means a lot to me!__

In Every Generation בכל-דור ודור

B'chol Dor Vador

Music and English Text: **Jeff Klepper** and **Dan Freelander**
Hebrew Text: adapted from the *Haggadah*

From the album *In Every Generation*

2. D G F C Am7 D7
D.S. al Coda
yim, b'-chol dor va - dor. 3. B' -
CODA
BRIDGE
D G C C/B Am D7 G
come a bet - ter day. B' - chol dor va - dor, a - nu
C C/B Am D7 G D/F♯ Em C G/B
cha - ya - vim lir - ot et atz - mei - nu, k' - i - lu a - nach - nu, a -
F Em Am Am/B Am/C Am/C♯ D7
nach - nu ya - tza - nu mi - Mitz - ra - yim. B' -
VERSE 4
G C G Am
chol dor va - dor in ev - ery gen - er - a - tion, we must look up - on our-selves as if from
D C G Em C G
slav-'ry we were freed. B' - chol dor va - dor, in ev - ery gen - er - a - tion, we must
Am D G Am
look a - round and help all the ones who are in need. We must look a - round and help all the

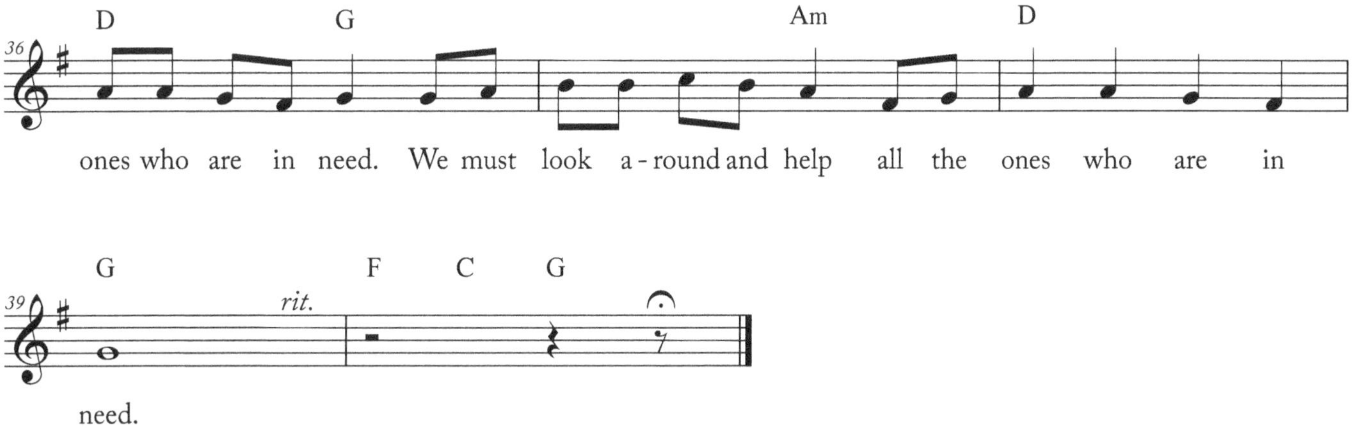

In each and every generation,
a person is obligated to see themselves
as if they left Egypt.

בְּכָל־דּוֹר וָדוֹר
חַיָּב אָדָם לִרְאוֹת אֶת־עַצְמוֹ
כְּאִלּוּ הוּא יָצָא מִמִּצְרָיִם.

In every generation,
each of us must see ourselves
as if we ourselves came out of Egypt.

בְּכָל־דּוֹר וָדוֹר
אָנוּ חַיָּבִים לִרְאוֹת אֶת־עַצְמֵנוּ,
כְּאִלּוּ אֲנַחְנוּ יָצָאנוּ מִמִּצְרָיִם.

In the Beginning

Music and text: **Jeff Klepper**

C D G D
fill the sea and sky. On the sixth day wom-an and man be-came God's
G C A7 G
part - ners for all time. And on Shab-bat God's
D C D G
work was done, it was time to take a rest. We re - mem - ber God's cre -
D G Em C A7
D.C. al Coda
a - tion on this spe - cial day of ho - li - ness.
CODA
D Bm
In the be - gin - ning God cre - a - ted the
G B♭ C D
heav - ens and the earth in the be - gin - ning
Bm B♭ C D
rit.
God cre - a - ted the heav- ens and the earth.

In This Place

Music and text: **Jeff Klepper**

From the album *In This Place*
To purchase multiple copies for your ensemble, please visit TranscontinentalMusic.com

994055

G Bm A7 D D7
A C♯m B7 E E7
far a-way from home, think-ing of my fam-i-ly, so hard to be a-
G Bm A7 D D7 G
A C♯m B7 E E7 A
lone. I was wres-tl-ing with feel-ings, I was try-ing not to show.
CHORUS
D A7 C Bm G C D A7 C Bm G
E B7 D C♯m A D E B7 D C♯m A
God was in this place and I, I did not know. God was in this place and I,
D G/D D G/D D G/D D
E A/E E A/E E A/E E
sim.
I did not know. There is a
BRIDGE
G Bm G Bm
A C♯m A C♯m
lad-der to the hea-vens. You must climb it if you can. You can
G Bm C Bm Em A7
A C♯m D C♯m F♯m B7
freely
do it, if you dream it. If you o-pen up your hand. 3. We are

VERSE 3
on this road to - geth - er, we are tra - vel - ling some - where. We are
all in need of com - fort, we could use some love and care. I can
still hear Ja - cob cal - ling from the To - rah long a - go.
rall.
CHORUS
a tempo
God was in this place and I, I did not know. God was in this place and
I, I did not know, I did not know.
sim.
rit.

Jeff's Nigun

Music: **Jeff Klepper**

From the album *We Are Partners*

Jonah

Music: **Jeff Klepper**
Text: **Jeff Klepper** and **Jeff Salkin**

Originally from the album *Bible People* (ARE) – From the Kol B'Seder album *Songs for Growin'*
To purchase multiple copies for your ensemble, please visit TranscontinentalMusic.com

G C F C G C D.S.
now we're in hot wa - ter and the on - ly way to stop it is to throw me in the sea."
VERSE 3
G C F C G C
3. A gi - ant fish was wait - ing and swal-lowed Mis - ter Jo - nah. He
F C D7 G F C
cried a - loud to God for three whole days and nights. Then the whale spat him up and
G C F C G C D.S.
Jo - nah went to Nin-e-veh.__ He told the Nin - e - vin - i - ans, "You bet - ter do what's right!"
VERSE 4
G C F C G C
4. The peo - ple all re - pent - ed, but Jo - nah was - n't sat - is - fied.__ He
F C D7 G F C
said to God, "You should-n't have for - giv - en ev - ery - one." Then God taught him a les - son that
G C F C G C D.S. al Fine
each of us should fol - low by look-ing at our-selves and the deeds that we have done.

Ki Anu Amecha כי אנו עמך

Music: **Jeff Klepper**
Text: Yom Kippur liturgy

From the album *We Are Partners*
Also available with piano accompaniment in *High Holy Days Anthology Volume I* (TMP 994043).
To purchase multiple copies for your ensemble, please visit TranscontinentalMusic.com

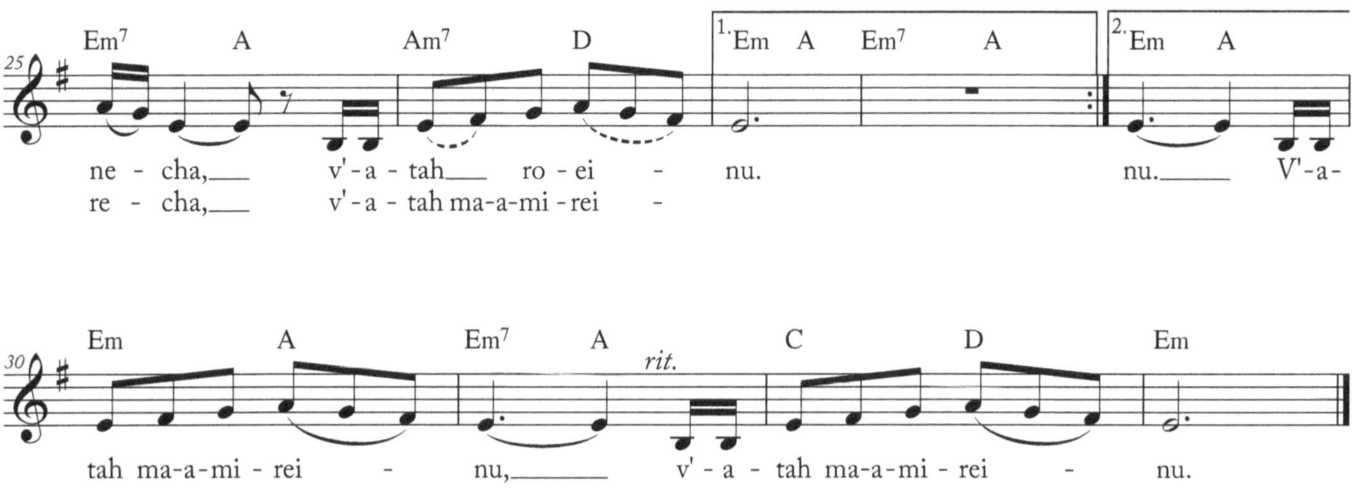

We are Your people; and You are our God.	כִּי אָנוּ עַמֶּךָ, וְאַתָּה אֱלֹהֵינוּ,
We are Your children, and You are our father, our mother.	אָנוּ בָנֶיךָ, וְאַתָּה אָבִינוּ.
We are the people who serve You; and You call us to serve.	אָנוּ עֲבָדֶיךָ, וְאַתָּה אֲדוֹנֵנוּ,
We are Your community; and You are our portion.	אָנוּ קְהָלֶךָ, וְאַתָּה חֶלְקֵנוּ.
We are Your legacy; and You are our purpose.	אָנוּ נַחֲלָתֶךָ, וְאַתָּה גוֹרָלֵנוּ,
We are Your flock; and You are our shepherd.	אָנוּ צֹאנֶךָ, וְאַתָּה רוֹעֵנוּ.
We are Your vineyard; and You watch over us.	אָנוּ כַרְמֶךָ, וְאַתָּה נוֹטְרֵנוּ,
We are Your work; and You are our maker.	אָנוּ פְעֻלָּתֶךָ, וְאַתָּה יוֹצְרֵנוּ.
We are Your beloved; and You are our lover.	אָנוּ רַעְיָתֶךָ, וְאַתָּה דוֹדֵנוּ,
We are Your treasure; and You are the one we cherish.	אָנוּ סְגֻלָּתֶךָ, וְאַתָּה קְרוֹבֵנוּ.
We are Your people; and You reign over us.	אָנוּ עַמֶּךָ, וְאַתָּה מַלְכֵּנוּ,
We offer You our words; and You offer us Yours.	אָנוּ מַאֲמִירֶיךָ, וְאַתָּה מַאֲמִירֵנוּ.

The Kippah Song

Music: **Jeff Klepper**
Text: **Jeff Klepper** and **Susan Nanus**

Originally from the album *Especially Jewish Symbols* (ARE) – From the Kol B'Seder album *Songs for Growin'*

CHORUS
G D G A D Em A
Kip - pah, yar - mul - kah, shows the world you're a
D D7 G A F♯m Bm
Jew. Wear it all day, or just when you pray, it's
Em A D 1. A D A7
to - tal - ly up to you. 3. You can
2. B7 Em A D
It's to - tal - ly up to you.

K'shoshanah

כשושנה

Music: **Jeff Klepper**
Text: Song of Songs 2:2-3

From the album *Yom Chadash*
To purchase multiple copies for your ensemble, please visit TranscontinentalMusic.com

 994055

כְּשׁוֹשַׁנָּה בֵּין הַחוֹחִים
כֵּן רַעְיָתִי בֵּין הַבָּנוֹת.
כְּתַפּוּחַ בַּעֲצֵי הַיַּעַר
כֵּן דּוֹדִי בֵּין הַבָּנִים.

Like a lily among thorns,
So is my darling among the maidens.
Like an apple tree among trees of the forest,
So is my beloved among the youths.

Laasok B'divrei Torah

לעסוק בדברי תורה

Music: **Jeff Klepper**
Text: Liturgy

From the album *Sparks of Torah*
To purchase multiple copies for your ensemble, please visit TranscontinentalMusic.com

994055

Blessed are You, Adonai our God,	בָּרוּךְ אַתָּה, יְיָ,
Sovereign of the universe,	אֱלֹהֵינוּ מֶלֶךְ הָעוֹלָם,
who hallows us with mitzvot,	אֲשֶׁר קִדְּשָׁנוּ בְּמִצְוֹתָיו
commanding us to engage with words of Torah.	וְצִוָּנוּ לַעֲסוֹק בְּדִבְרֵי תוֹרָה.

Lailah Tov

לילה טוב

Music and text: **Jeff Klepper** and **Rachel Klepper**

Good night.

.לַיְלָה טוֹב

From the album *We Are Partners*
To purchase multiple copies for your ensemble, please visit TranscontinentalMusic.com

 994055

Lamdeini Elohai

למדני אלוהי

Teach Me to Pray

Music: **Jeff Klepper**
Text: **Lea Goldberg**

From the album *Yom Chadash*

Teach me, O God, a blessing, a prayer
on the mystery of a withered leaf,
on ripened fruit so fair,
on the freedom
to see, to sense, to breathe,
to know, to hope, to despair.

לַמְּדֵנִי, אֱלֹהַי, בָּרֵךְ וְהִתְפַּלֵּל
עַל סוֹד עָלֶה קָמֵל,
עַל נֹגַהּ פְּרִי בָּשֵׁל,
עַל הַחֵרוּת הַזֹּאת:
לִרְאוֹת, לָחוּשׁ, לִנְשֹׁם,
לָדַעַת, לְיַחֵל, לְהִכָּשֵׁל.

Teach my lips a blessing,
a hymn of praise,
as each morning
and night
You renew Your days,
lest my day today be as the one before;
lest routine set my ways.

לַמֵּד אֶת שִׂפְתוֹתַי
בְּרָכָה וְשִׁיר הַלֵּל,
בְּהִתְחַדֵּשׁ זְמַנְּךָ
עִם בֹּקֶר וְעִם לֵיל,
לְבַל יִהְיֶה יוֹמִי הַיּוֹם
כִּתְמוֹל שִׁלְשׁוֹם,
לְבַל יִהְיֶה עָלַי יוֹמִי הֶרְגֵּל.

L'chah Dodi

לכה דודי

Music: **Jeff Klepper**
Text: **Shlomo Alkabetz** (16th c.)

From the album *Songs for Growin'*
Also available for choir in *Jeff Klepper Anthology* (TMP 993117)
To purchase multiple copies for your ensemble, please visit TranscontinentalMusic.com

VERSES
Am
echo
Em
echo
mor v'-za-chor b'-di-bur e-chad hish-mi-
rat Sha-bat l' - chu v'-neil-chah, ki
o - r'-ri, hit - o - r'-ri, ki
i v'-sha-lom a - te-ret ba-lah, gam
D
echo
Em
echo
a - nu Eil ham'-yu-chad, A-do-
hi m'-kor ha - b' - ra-chah, mei-
va o-reich, ku - mi o - ri, u-
b'-sim-chah uv - tzo - ho-lah, toch
Am
echo
Em
echo
nai e-chad u-sh-mo e-chad, l'-
rosh mi-ke-dem n' - su - chah, sof
ri u-ri shir da - bei-ri, k'-
e-mu-nei am s'-gu-lah, bo-
C
D
Am7
B7
1.-3. repeat
4. D.S. al Fine
sheim ul - tif - e - ret v' - li - t'hi - lah. L'-
ma - a-seh b'-ma - cha - sha - vah t'chi - lah.
vod A - do - nai a - la - yich nig - lah.
i cha - lah, bo - i cha - lah.

לְכָה דוֹדִי לִקְרַאת כַּלָּה,
פְּנֵי שַׁבָּת נְקַבְּלָה.

Beloved, come to meet the bride;
beloved, come to greet Shabbat.

1. שָׁמוֹר וְזָכוֹר בְּדִבּוּר אֶחָד,
הִשְׁמִיעָנוּ אֵל הַמְיֻחָד,
יְיָ אֶחָד וּשְׁמוֹ אֶחָד,
לְשֵׁם וּלְתִפְאֶרֶת וְלִתְהִלָּה.

1. "Keep" and "remember": a single command
the Only God caused us to hear;
the Eternal is One, God's name is One;
glory and praise are God's.

2. לִקְרַאת שַׁבָּת לְכוּ וְנֵלְכָה,
כִּי הִיא מְקוֹר הַבְּרָכָה,
מֵרֹאשׁ מִקֶּדֶם נְסוּכָה,
סוֹף מַעֲשֶׂה בְּמַחֲשָׁבָה תְּחִלָּה.

2. Come with me to meet Shabbat,
forever a fountain of blessing.
Still it flows, as from the start:
the last of days, for which the first was made.

5. הִתְעוֹרְרִי, הִתְעוֹרְרִי,
כִּי בָא אוֹרֵךְ, קוּמִי אוֹרִי,
עוּרִי עוּרִי, שִׁיר דַּבֵּרִי,
כְּבוֹד יְיָ עָלַיִךְ נִגְלָה.

5. Awake, awake,
your light has come!
Arise, shine, awake, and sing:
the Eternal's glory dawns upon you.

9. בּוֹאִי בְשָׁלוֹם עֲטֶרֶת בַּעְלָהּ,
גַּם בְּשִׂמְחָה וּבְצָהֳלָה,
תּוֹךְ אֱמוּנֵי עַם סְגֻלָּה,
בּוֹאִי כַלָּה, בּוֹאִי כַלָּה.

9. Enter in peace, O crown of your husband;
enter in gladness, enter in joy.
Come to the people that keeps its faith.
Enter, O bride! Enter, O bride!

L’chu N’ran’nah

לכו נרננה

Music: **Jeff Klepper**
Text: Psalm 95:1-2

Come, let us sing joyously to Adonai,
raise a shout for our Rock and Deliverer.
Let us come into God's presence with praise;
let us raise a shout for God in song!

לְכוּ נְרַנְּנָה לַייָ,
נָרִיעָה לְצוּר יִשְׁעֵנוּ.
נְקַדְּמָה פָנָיו בְּתוֹדָה,
בִּזְמִרוֹת נָרִיעַ לוֹ.

From the album *We Are Partners*
Also available with piano accompaniment in *Jeff Klepper Anthology* (TMP 993117).
To purchase multiple copies for your ensemble, please visit TranscontinentalMusic.com

Leidah Hi Reishit לידה היא ראשית

Birth Is a Beginning

Music: **Jeff Klepper**
English text: **Alvin Fine**
Hebrew translation: **Simeon Maslin**

From the album *In This Place*

Em Dm B♭ G(sus4) G
v' - a - na, liv - ri - ut cha - za - rah. Mei-a - vei -
Am C Am Em F
rah lim - chi - lah, mib' - di - dut li - di-dut, mi-sim-chah l' - to - dah,
Em F Em Dm
mi-yi - su - rim l' - ra - cha-mim, mi - ya - gon, la-ha - va -
Em Dm G(sus4) C F(add2) C F(add2)
nah, mei-ei - mah le - e - mu - nah. Lei-
D C Am Dm G(sus4)
dah hi rei - shit uf - ti - rah, tach - lit, v' - ha - cha-yim
C C/B Am Am/G F G Am
k'ma-sa heim, a - li-yah k'do - shah, sha - lav a-char sha-lav,
Em F Em Dm Em
sha - lav a-char sha-lav, mi - lei-dah, lif - ti - rah,
Dm Em B♭ F C
l'-cha - yei o - lam ha - ba.

לידה היא ראשית

LEIDAH HI REISHIT (BIRTH IS A BEGINNING)

Birth is a beginning,
And death a destination;
But life is a journey,
A going—a growing
From stage to stage.

From childhood to maturity
And youth to age.
From innocence to awareness
And ignorance to knowing;
From follishness to discretion
And then perhaps to wisdom.

From weakness to strength
Or strength to weakness—
And, often, back again.
From health to sickness
And back, we pray, to health again.

From offense to forgiveness,
From loneliness to love,
From joy to gratitude,
From pain to compassion,
And grief to understanding—
From fear to faith.

Birth is a beginning,
And death a destination;
But life is a journey,
A sacred pilgrimage
Made stage by stage—
From birth to death
To life everlasting.

לֵידָה הִיא רֵאשִׁית
וּפְטִירָה—תַּכְלִית.
וְהַחַיִּים כְּמַסָּע הֵם:
כַּהֲלִיכָה, כִּצְמִיחָה
מִשָּׁלָב לְשָׁלָב.

מִיַּלְדוּת לְבַגְרוּת,
מִנֹּעַר לְשֵׂיבָה.
מִתְּמִימוּת לְדַעַת,
מִבּוּרוּת לְבִינָה;
מִטִּפְּשׁוּת לְשִׁפּוּט
וְאָז—אוּלַי—לְחָכְמָה.

מֵחֻלְשָׁה לְעָצְמָה
אוֹ עָצְמָה לַחֻלְשָׁה—
וּלְעִתִּים בַּחֲזָרָה.
מִבְּרִיאוּת לְמַחֲלָה,
וְאָנָּא, לִבְרִיאוּת חֲזָרָה.

מֵעֲבֵרָה לִמְחִילָה,
מִבְּדִידוּת לִידִידוּת,
מִשִּׂמְחָה לְתוֹדָה,
מִיִּסּוּרִים לְרַחֲמִים,
מִיָּגוֹן לַהֲבָנָה—
מֵאֵימָה לֶאֱמוּנָה.

לֵידָה הִיא רֵאשִׁית
וּפְטִירָה—תַּכְלִית.
וְהַחַיִּים כְּמַסָּע הֵם—
עֲלִיָּה קְדוֹשָׁה,
שָׁלָב אַחַר שָׁלָב—
מִלֵּידָה לִפְטִירָה,
לְחַיֵּי עוֹלָם הַבָּא.

Lirdof Tzedek

לרדוף צדק

Blessing for Social Justice

Music: **Jeff Klepper**
Text: Social action blessing

From the album *We Are Partners*
To purchase multiple copies for your ensemble, please visit TranscontinentalMusic.com

994055

לרדוף צדק

LIRDOF TZEDEK
(BLESSING FOR SOCIAL JUSTICE)

בָּרוּךְ אַתָּה, יְיָ, אֱלֹהֵינוּ מֶלֶךְ הָעוֹלָם,
אֲשֶׁר קִדְּשָׁנוּ בְּמִצְוֹתָיו וְצִוָּנוּ
לִרְדֹּף צֶדֶק.

We praise You, Eternal God.
You have made us holy with your commandments
and have commanded us to pursue justice.

Lo Alecha

לא עליך

Music: **Jeff Klepper** and **Dan Freelander**
Hebrew text: *Pirkei Avot* 2:16
English text: **Jeff Klepper**

It is not your duty to complete the work.
Neither are you free to desist from it.

לֹא עָלֶיךָ הַמְּלָאכָה לִגְמוֹר
וְלֹא אַתָּה בֶן חוֹרִין לְהִבָּטֵל מִמֶּנָּה.

Originally from the album *Songs NFTY Sings* – From the Kol B'Seder album *In Every Generation*
To purchase multiple copies for your ensemble, please visit TranscontinentalMusic.com

994055

Lo Bashamayim Hi לא בשמים הוא

Music and English text: **Jeff Klepper**
Hebrew text: Deuteronomy 30:12-14

From the album *In Every Generation*
To purchase multiple copies for your ensemble, please visit TranscontinentalMusic.com

Am F G Last time to Coda Am
- cha ha - da - var m' - od, m' - od.
D Am D rit. C Am7 relaxed
The To - rah's
D(add4sus2)/A Am7 D(add4sus2)/A Am7 D(add4sus2)/A Am7 D(add4sus2)/A
not in heav - en, it's not a - cross the sea. The
Am7 D(add4sus2)/A Am7 D(add4sus2)/A Am7 D(add4sus2)/A
words are ver - y near and clear, for ev - ery - one to
Am accel. D G G(sus4) stronger G
see. They're in your mouth and in your mind.
Am G Em
They're in your heart, there for you to find.
Am G G(sus4) G Am
It's not too far, it's not un - clear.
G Em Am D.S. al Coda non-riten.
It's not out there, it's ver - y, ver - y near! Ki ka -

𝄌 CODA

It is not in the heavens,
neither is it beyond the sea.
No, the thing is very close to you.

לֹא בַשָּׁמַיִם הִוא,
וְלֹא־מֵעֵבֶר לַיָּם הִוא.
כִּי־קָרוֹב אֵלֶיךָ הַדָּבָר מְאֹד.

Maariv Aravim מַעֲרִיב עֲרָבִים

Music: **Jeff Klepper**
Text: Evening liturgy

Praised are You, Adonai our God,
Ruler of the universe,
who speaks the evening into being.

בָּרוּךְ אַתָּה, יְיָ,
אֱלֹהֵינוּ מֶלֶךְ הָעוֹלָם,
אֲשֶׁר בִּדְבָרוֹ מַעֲרִיב עֲרָבִים.

From the album *Songs for Growin'*
Also available with piano accompaniment in *Jeff Klepper Anthology* (TMP 993117).
To purchase multiple copies for your ensemble, please visit TranscontinentalMusic.com

Mah Tovu

מה-טבו

Music: **Jeff Klepper**
Text: Numbers 24:5; Psalms 5:8, 26:8, 69:14

Originally from the album *Songs NFTY Sings* – From the Kol B'Seder album *Sparks of Torah*
Choral and accompanied versions available on TranscontinentalMusic.com
To purchase multiple copies for your ensemble, please visit TranscontinentalMusic.com

C#m F# G D E(sus4) E
Em A B♭ F G(sus4) G
D.C.
chal kod - sh' - cha b' - yir - a - te - cha.
VERSE 2
C#m F# C#m F# G
Em A Em A B♭
(2.) nai, a - hav - ti m' - on bei - te - cha, u - m - kom mish -
D E(sus4) E C#m F#
F G(sus4) G Em A
kan k' - vo - de - cha. Va - a - ni esh - ta - cha - veh v' -
C#m F# G D E(sus4) E
Em A B♭ F G(sus4) G
D.C.
ech - ra - ah, ev - r' - chah lif - nei A - do - nai o - si.
VERSE 3
C#m F# C#m F# G
Em A Em A B♭
(3.) ni t' - fi - la - ti l' - cha, A - do - nai,
D E(sus4) E C#m F# C#m
F G(sus4) G Em A Em
eit ra - tzon. E - lo - him, b' - rov chas -
F# G D E(sus4) E
A B♭ F G(sus4) G
D.C. al Coda
de - cha, a - nei - ni be - e - met yish - e - cha.

𝄌 CODA

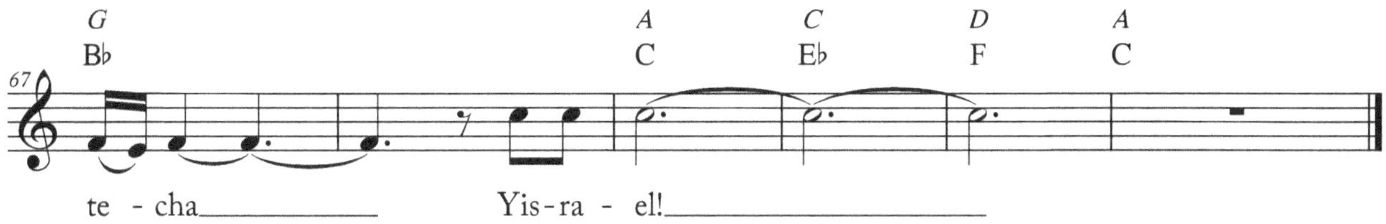

How fair are your tents, O Jacob,
your dwellings, O Israel!

מַה־טֹּבוּ אֹהָלֶיךָ, יַעֲקֹב,
מִשְׁכְּנֹתֶיךָ, יִשְׂרָאֵל!

I, through Your abundant love,
enter Your house;
I bow down in awe
at Your holy temple.

וַאֲנִי בְּרֹב חַסְדְּךָ
אָבוֹא בֵיתֶךָ,
אֶשְׁתַּחֲוֶה אֶל־הֵיכַל קָדְשְׁךָ
בְּיִרְאָתֶךָ.

Adonai, I love Your temple abode,
the dwelling-place of Your glory.

יְיָ, אָהַבְתִּי מְעוֹן בֵּיתֶךָ,
וּמְקוֹם מִשְׁכַּן כְּבוֹדֶךָ.

I will humbly bow down low
before Adonai, my Maker.

וַאֲנִי אֶשְׁתַּחֲוֶה וְאֶכְרָעָה,
אֶבְרְכָה לִפְנֵי־יְיָ עֹשִׂי.

As for me, may my prayer come to You,
Adonai, at a favorable time.
O God, in Your abundant faithfulness,
answer me with Your sure deliverance.

וַאֲנִי תְפִלָּתִי לְךָ, יְיָ,
עֵת רָצוֹן.
אֱלֹהִים, בְּרָב־חַסְדֶּךָ,
עֲנֵנִי בֶּאֱמֶת יִשְׁעֶךָ.

The Mezuzah Song

Music: **Jeff Klepper**
Text: **Jeff Klepper** and **Susan Nanus**

Originally from the album *Especially Jewish Symbols* (ARE) – From the Kol B'Seder album *Songs for Growin'*
To purchase multiple copies for your ensemble, please visit TranscontinentalMusic.com

Mi Amar

מי אמר

Music: **Jeff Klepper**
Text: **Tzeira Trifon**

From the album *Yom Chadash*

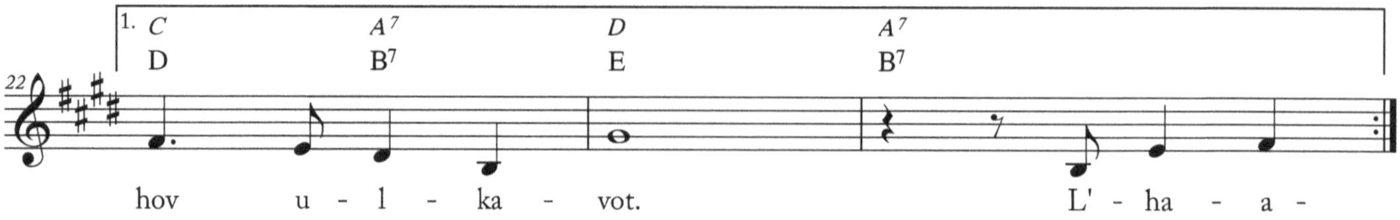

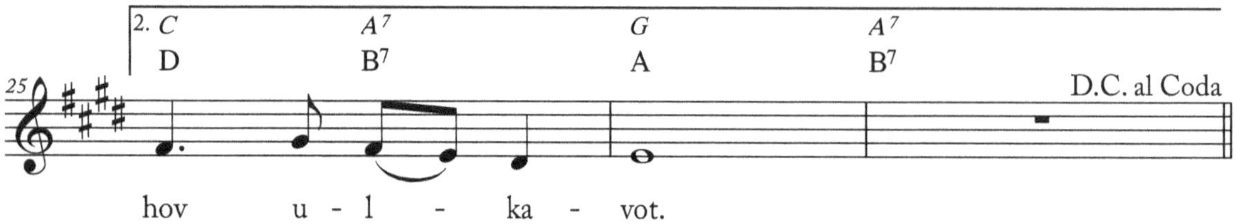

CODA

Who says that it's impossible
to arise to a new day,
to swallow light to the sound of a bird,
to gather a spoon of honey?
Who says that it's impossible
to rise up and to love,
to embrace everything, to sing out loud,
to believe in goodness?

מִי אָמַר שֶׁאִי אֶפְשָׁר
לָקוּם אֶל יוֹם חָדָשׁ
לִגְמוֹעַ אוֹר לְקוֹל צִפּוֹר
וְלֶאֱרוֹת כַּף דְּבָשׁ?
מִי זֶה אָמַר שֶׁאִי אֶפְשָׁר
לָקוּם וְלֶאֱהוֹב
לַחֲבוֹק הַכֹּל לָשִׁיר בְּקוֹל
לְהַאֲמִין שֶׁטּוֹב?

To believe in goodness, to cause pain to surrender,
to feel and to experience, to love and to hope.

לְהַאֲמִין שֶׁטּוֹב לְהַכְנִיעַ כָּל מַכְאוֹב
לְהַרְגִּישׁ וְלַחֲווֹת לֶאֱהוֹב וּלְקַוּוֹת.

Those who say,
"Perhaps tomorrow and not right now"
have not yet dreamed...
We'll teach them how to dream!

מִי שֶׁאָמַר
"אוּלַי מָחָר" וְלֹא "מַמָּשׁ הַיּוֹם"
הוּא מֵעוֹלָם עוֹד לֹא חָלַם,
לַמְּדוּהוּ אֵיךְ לַחֲלוֹם!

Mi Chamochah

מי-כמוכה

Music: **Jeff Klepper**
Text: Evening liturgy

From the album *Yom Chadash*
Also available with piano accompaniment in *Jeff Klepper Anthology* (TMP 993117).
To purchase multiple copies for your ensemble, please visit TranscontinentalMusic.com

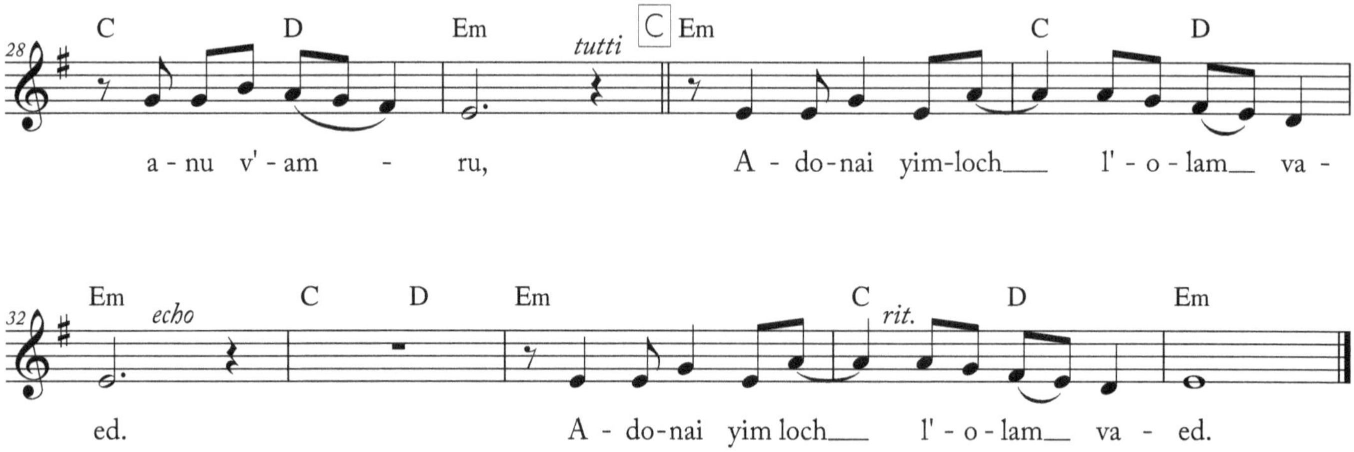

Who is like You, O God, among the gods that are worshiped?	מִי־כָמֹכָה בָּאֵלִם יְיָ!
Who is like You, majestic in holiness,	מִי כָּמֹכָה נֶאְדָּר בַּקֹּדֶשׁ,
awesome in splendor, working wonders?	נוֹרָא תְהִלֹּת, עֹשֵׂה פֶלֶא!
Your children witnessed Your sovereignty,	מַלְכוּתְךָ רָאוּ בָנֶיךָ,
the sea splitting before Moses and Miriam.	בּוֹקֵעַ יָם לִפְנֵי מֹשֶׁה וּמִרְיָם.
"This is our God!" they cried.	זֶה אֵלִי, עָנוּ וְאָמְרוּ,
"Adonai will reign forever and ever!"	יְיָ יִמְלֹךְ לְעוֹלָם וָעֶד!

Modeh Ani

מודה אני

Music: **Jeff Klepper** and **Dan Freelander**
Text: Morning liturgy

I offer thanks to You,
ever-living Sovereign (Spirit),
that You have restored my soul to me in mercy:
How great is Your trust.

מוֹדֶה / מוֹדָה אֲנִי לְפָנֶיךָ,
מֶלֶךְ / רוּחַ חַי וְקַיָּם,
שֶׁהֶחֱזַרְתָּ בִּי נִשְׁמָתִי בְּחֶמְלָה,
רַבָּה אֱמוּנָתֶךָ.

Modim Anachnu Lach מודים אנחנו לך

Music and English text: **Jeff Klepper**
Hebrew text: Evening liturgy

We acknowledge You with thanks. מוֹדִים אֲנַֽחְנוּ לָךְ.

From the album *In This Place*
Choral and accompanied versions availabe on TranscontinentalMusic.com
To purchase multiple copies for your ensemble, please visit TranscontinentalMusic.com

994055

My Sukkah

Music and text: **Jeff Klepper** and **Dan Freelander**

From the album *Songs for Growin'*

CODA

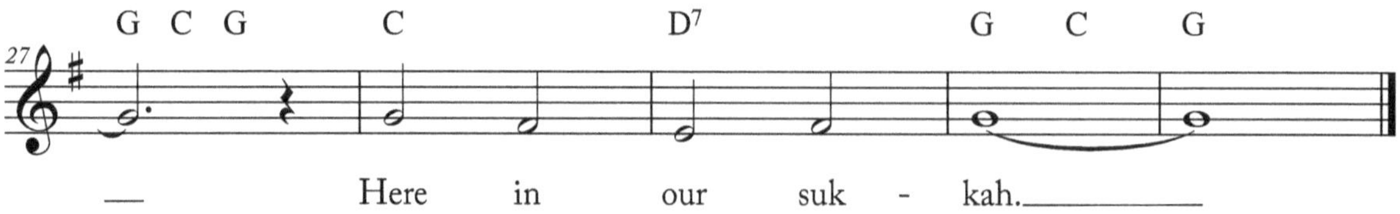

Welcome.

בְּרוּכִים הַבָּאִים.

Open Up Our Eyes

Music and text: **Jeff Klepper**

From the album *In This Place*
Also available with piano accompaniment in *Jeff Klepper Anthology* (TMP 993117).
To purchase multiple copies for your ensemble, please visit TranscontinentalMusic.com

Or Zarua

אור זרע

Music: **Jeff Klepper**
Text: Psalm 97:11

Light is sown for the righteous, joy for the upright.

אוֹר זָרֻעַ לַצַּדִּיק וּלְיִשְׁרֵי־לֵב שִׂמְחָה.

From the album *Snapshots Vol. 1*
Also available with piano accompaniment in *Jeff Klepper Anthology* (TMP 993117).
To purchase multiple copies for your ensemble, please visit TranscontinentalMusic.com

Oseh Shalom עושה שלום

Music: **Jeff Klepper**
Text: Liturgy

May the One who makes peace in the high heavens
make peace for us,
for all Israel and all who inhabit the earth.
Amen.

עֹשֶׂה שָׁלוֹם בִּמְרוֹמָיו,
הוּא יַעֲשֶׂה שָׁלוֹם עָלֵינוּ,
וְעַל כָּל יִשְׂרָאֵל, וְעַל כָּל יוֹשְׁבֵי תֵבֵל,
וְאִמְרוּ: אָמֵן.

Originally from the album *Songs NFTY Sings* – From the Kol B'Seder album *The Bridge*
Choral and accompanied versions available on TranscontinentalMusic.com
To purchase multiple copies for your ensemble, please visit TranscontinentalMusic.com

Planting Song

Music: **Jeff Klepper**
Text: **Jeff Klepper** and **Dan Castellaneta**

From the album *Songs for Growin'*

VERSE 2
E A
(2.) To - rah it is writ-ten, when we saw the prom-ised land, we
F♯m C♯m A B7
plant - ed trees at ev - ery turn, for this was God's com-mand. And to -
E A
day in mo-dern Is - rael where they made the des-ert bloom, in
F♯m C♯m A B7 D.S.
such a ti - ny coun-try for a tree there's al - ways room! So
VERSE 3
E A F♯m
(3.) Tal - mud is a say-ing writ-ten man-y years a - go. Ev-ery plant has a
C♯m F♯m7 B7 E
spe-cial star to teach it how to grow. So if you hap - pen to be
A F♯m C♯m
plant-ing and some-one comes a-long fin-ish what you're do-ing and to-
CODA
A B7 D.S. al Coda
geth - er sing this song! So
A B7 E
branch - es all a - round!

Pursuer of Peace

Music and English text: **Jeff Klepper**
Hebrew text: *Pirkei Avot* 1:14

From the album *We Are Partners*
To purchase multiple copies for your ensemble, please visit TranscontinentalMusic.com

 994055

And if not now, when?

וְאִם לֹא עַכְשָׁיו, אֵימָתַי?

Rabbi Ben Bag Bag

Music: **Jeff Klepper**
Text: **Jeff Klepper**, based on *Pirkei Avot* 5:22

From the album *Jeff Klepper Live in Concert*
To purchase multiple copies for your ensemble, please visit TranscontinentalMusic.com

994055

C(add9) Am7 D(sus4) D
and I hope you sing a - long.
He would turn to them and say:
and now it's in a song!
You've got to
CHORUS
G Am Em D C
turn it, turn it, turn it a - gain. Turn it a - round your
Em D G Am Em D
mind. You've got to turn it, turn it, turn it a - gain. You'll
C Am7 D(sus4) 1.2. D7
nev - er know what se - crets you might find!
2. For Rab - bi Ben
3. For Rab - bi Ben
3. D7
END
G Am Em D G Am
You've got to turn it, turn it, turn it a - gain. Turn it, turn it,
Em D G Am Em D
turn it a - gain. Turn it, turn it, turn it a - gain.

Ruth and Naomi

Music and text: **Jeff Klepper** and **Dan Freelander**

From the album *Sparks of Torah*
To purchase multiple copies for your ensemble, please visit TranscontinentalMusic.com

D Em C Em
that's where I will go. And wher-ev - er you are,
C D D7 C
that's where I will be. Your peo - ple shall be my
G(sus4) G G/F♯ Em C Am D
peo - ple, and your God shall be my God.
D7 C G(sus4) G G/F♯
Your peo - ple shall be my peo - ple,
Em C F G
Fine
and your God shall be my God."
VERSE 2
G G/F♯ Em
2. All the choic-es we make and the lives that we lead are re -
C Bm C
flec-tions of how we have grown. Ruth made a choice when she
Am C D(sus4) D7
D.S. al Fine
cast her lot with our fam -'ly and found a new home. "Do not urge,

Shabbat HaMalkah שבת המלכה

Music: **Jeff Klepper**
Text: **Chaim Nachman Bialik**

Commissioned in honor of Rabbi Rosalind Gold

From the album *We Are Partners*
Choral and accompanied versions available on TranscontinentalMusic.com
To purchase multiple copies for your ensemble, please visit TranscontinentalMusic.com

הַחַמָּה מֵרֹאשׁ הָאִילָנוֹת נִסְתַּלְּקָה,
בֹּאוּ וְנֵצֵא לִקְרַאת שַׁבָּת הַמַּלְכָּה.
הִנֵּה הִיא יוֹרֶדֶת, הַקְּדוֹשָׁה הַבְּרוּכָה.
וְעִמָּהּ מַלְאָכִים, צְבָא שָׁלוֹם וּמְנוּחָה.
בֹּאִי בֹּאִי הַמַּלְכָּה, בֹּאִי בֹּאִי הַכַּלָּה.
שָׁלוֹם עֲלֵיכֶם, מַלְאֲכֵי הַשָּׁלוֹם.

The sun has already disappeared beyond the treetops,
Come let us go and welcome the Sabbath Queen,
She is already descending among us, holy and blessed,
And with her are angels, a host of peace and rest,
Come, O Queen, Come, O Queen,
Peace be unto you, O Angels of Peace.

English translation by Chaim Nachman Bialik

Shalom Rav שלום רב

Music: **Jeff Klepper** and **Dan Freelander**
Text: Liturgy

Originally from the album *Songs NFTY Sings* – From the Kol B'Seder album *Snapshots Vol. 1*
Choral and accompanied versions available on TranscontinentalMusic.com
To purchase multiple copies for your ensemble, please visit TranscontinentalMusic.com

𝄌 CODA

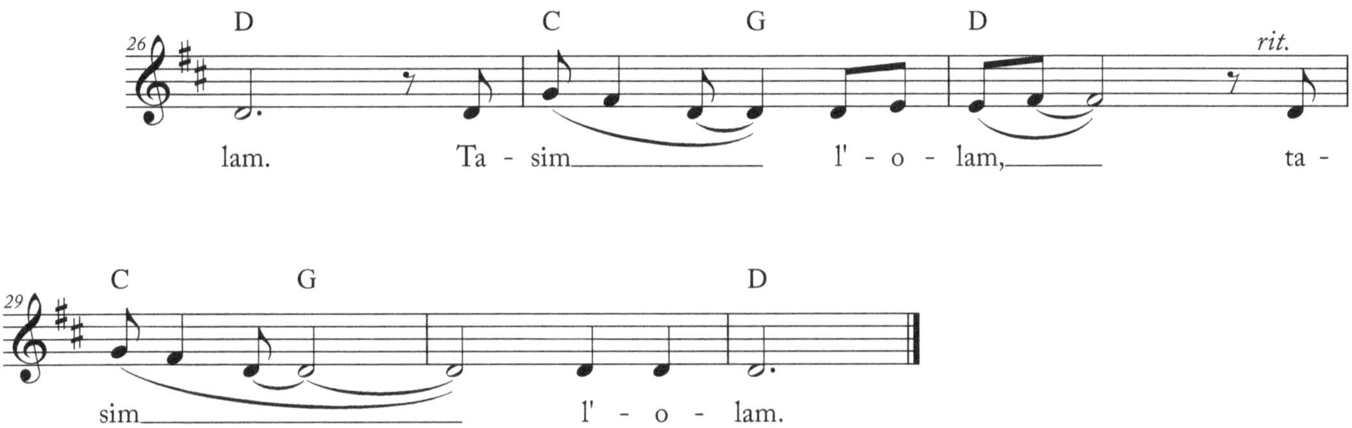

Grant abundant peace to Israel
Your people forever,
for You are the Sovereign God
of all peace.
May it be pleasing to You
to bless Your people Israel
in every season and moment with Your peace.

שָׁלוֹם רָב עַל יִשְׂרָאֵל עַמְּךָ
תָּשִׂים לְעוֹלָם,
כִּי אַתָּה הוּא מֶלֶךְ אָדוֹן
לְכָל הַשָּׁלוֹם.
וְטוֹב בְּעֵינֶיךָ לְבָרֵךְ
אֶת עַמְּךָ יִשְׂרָאֵל
בְּכָל עֵת וּבְכָל שָׁעָה בִּשְׁלוֹמֶךָ.

Shavua Tov, May You Have a Good Week שבוע טוב

Music: **Jeff Klepper**
Text: **Jeff Klepper** and **Susan Nanus**

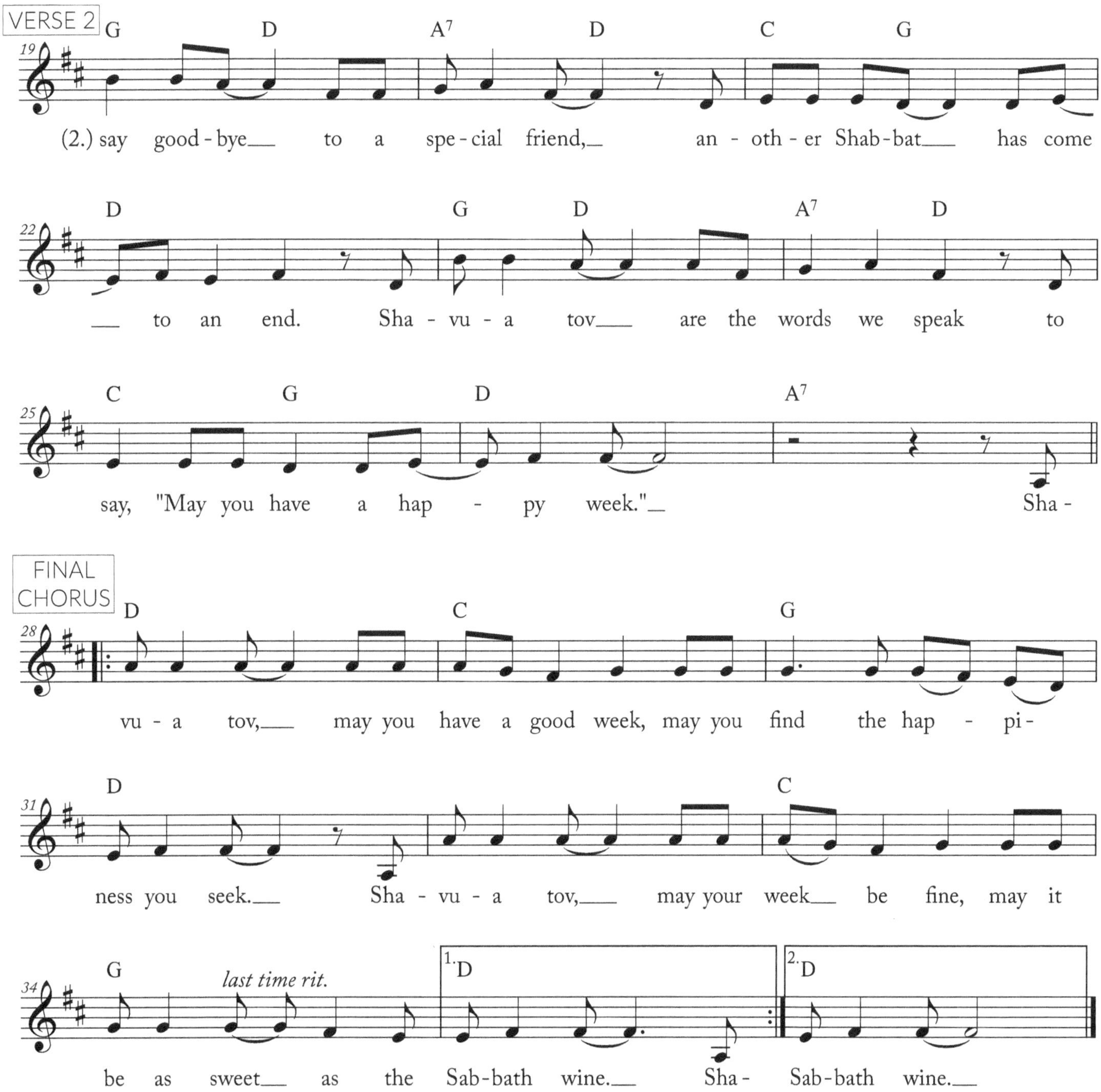

A good week...

...שָׁבוּעַ טוֹב

Shehecheyanu I שהחינו

Music: **Jeff Klepper**
Text: Liturgy

With motion ♩ = 116
For solo voice, three voices, or three-part choir
Suggested order: I - I/II - I/II/III - I/II/III

From the album *We Are Partners*
To purchase multiple copies for your ensemble, please visit TranscontinentalMusic.com

Blessed are You, Adonai our God,
Sovereign of all,
for giving us life, for sustaining us,
and for enabling us to reach this season.

בָּרוּךְ אַתָּה, יְיָ,
אֱלֹהֵינוּ מֶלֶךְ הָעוֹלָם,
שֶׁהֶחֱיָנוּ וְקִיְּמָנוּ
וְהִגִּיעָנוּ לַזְּמַן הַזֶּה.

Shehecheyanu II שהחינו

Thank You, God

Music and English text: **Jeff Klepper**
Hebrew text: Liturgy

Blessed are You, Adonai our God,
Sovereign of all,
for giving us life, for sustaining us,
and for enabling us to reach this season.

בָּרוּךְ אַתָּה, יְיָ,
אֱלֹהֵינוּ מֶלֶךְ הָעוֹלָם,
שֶׁהֶחֱיָנוּ וְקִיְּמָנוּ
וְהִגִּיעָנוּ לַזְּמַן הַזֶּה.

From the album *We Are Partners*
Also available with piano accompaniment in *Mikraei Kodesh Volume II* (TMP 994057).
To purchase multiple copies for your ensemble, please visit TranscontinentalMusic.com

Sh'ma Koleinu שמע קולנו

Music and English text: **Jeff Klepper**
Hebrew text: High Holy Day liturgy

From the album *In This Place*
To purchase multiple copies for your ensemble, please visit TranscontinentalMusic.com

Hear our call, Adonai our God.
Show us compassion.
Renew our days.

שְׁמַע קוֹלֵנוּ, יְיָ אֱלֹהֵינוּ.
חוּס וְרַחֵם עָלֵינוּ.
חַדֵּשׁ יָמֵינוּ.

Shomeir Yisrael

שומר ישראל

Music: **Jeff Klepper**
Text: Liturgy

From the album *We Are Partners*
To purchase multiple copies for your ensemble, please visit TranscontinentalMusic.com

Guardian of Israel,
guard the remnant of Israel.
Let Israel not perish,
those who say "Sh'ma Yisrael."

Guardian of the unique people,
guard the remnant of that people.
Let that people not perish,
those who proclaim
the Oneness of Your Name.

שׁוֹמֵר יִשְׂרָאֵל,
שְׁמוֹר שְׁאֵרִית יִשְׂרָאֵל,
וְאַל־יֹאבַד יִשְׂרָאֵל
הָאוֹמְרִים שְׁמַע יִשְׂרָאֵל.

שׁוֹמֵר גּוֹי אֶחָד
שְׁמוֹר שְׁאֵרִית עַם אֶחָד
וְאַל־יֹאבַד גּוֹי אֶחָד
הַמְיַחֲדִים שִׁמְךָ
יְיָ אֱלֹהֵינוּ, יְיָ אֶחָד.

Sim Shalom

שים שלום

Music: **Jeff Klepper**
Text: Liturgy

From the album *We Are Partners*

VERSE 2
C D C D G Em
(2.) or pa - ne - cha na - ta - ta la - nu, A - do - nai E - lo - hei - nu, To -
A C D C D
rat cha-yim v' - a - ha - vat che - sed, utz - da - kah uv - ra - chah v' - ra - cha -
C Em A D.S.
mim v' - cha - yim v' - sha - lom.
VERSE 3
G quieter F♯m Em D
(3.) tov bei - ne - cha l' - va - reich et am - cha Yis - ra - el b' -
G F♯m cresc. C A D.S. al Coda
chol eit u - v - chol sha - ah bish - lo - me - cha.
CODA
D G D C D G D C
Sim sha-lom to - vah uv-ra-chah, chein va-che - sed v' - ra - cha-mim,
D G D C rit. D C D
sim sha-lom to - vah uv - ra-chah, chein va - che-sed v' - ra - cha - mim.

שִׂים שָׁלוֹם טוֹבָה וּבְרָכָה,
חֵן וָחֶסֶד וְרַחֲמִים,
עָלֵינוּ וְעַל כָּל יִשְׂרָאֵל עַמֶּךָ.
בָּרְכֵנוּ, יוֹצְרֵנוּ (אָבִינוּ), כֻּלָּנוּ כְּאֶחָד
בְּאוֹר פָּנֶיךָ,
כִּי בְאוֹר פָּנֶיךָ נָתַתָּ לָּנוּ,
יְיָ אֱלֹהֵינוּ,
תּוֹרַת חַיִּים וְאַהֲבַת חֶסֶד,
וּצְדָקָה וּבְרָכָה וְרַחֲמִים
וְחַיִּים וְשָׁלוֹם.
וְטוֹב בְּעֵינֶיךָ לְבָרֵךְ אֶת־עַמְּךָ יִשְׂרָאֵל
בְּכָל עֵת וּבְכָל שָׁעָה בִּשְׁלוֹמֶךָ.

Grant peace, goodness and blessing,
grace, kindness and mercy,
to us and to all Your people Israel.
Bless us, our Creator, all of us together,
through the light of Your presence.
Truly through the light of Your presence,
Adonai our God,
You gave us a Torah of life—
the love of kindess, justice and blessing,
mercy, life, and peace.
May You see fit to bless Your people Israel
at all times, at every hour, with Your peace.

Sin'u Ra

שנאו-רע

Music: **Jeff Klepper** and **Dan Freelander**
Text: Amos 5:15; Leviticus 25:10

Originally from the album *Songs NFTY Sings* – From the Kol B'Seder album *Snapshots Vol. 1*

Hate evil and love good,
and establish justice in the gate.
You shall proclaim release throughout the land
for all its inhabitants.

שִׂנְאוּ־רָע וְאֶהֱבוּ טוֹב
וְהַצִּיגוּ בַשַּׁעַר מִשְׁפָּט.
וּקְרָאתֶם דְּרוֹר בָּאָרֶץ
לְכָל־יֹשְׁבֶיהָ.

The Synagogue

Music: **Jeff Klepper**
Text: **Jeff Klepper** and **Susan Nanus**

House of meeting... בֵּית כְּנֶסֶת...
House of prayer... בֵּית תְּפִלָּה...
House of study... בֵּית הַמִּדְרָשׁ...

Ten Commandments

Music: **Jeff Klepper**
Text: **Jeff Klepper** and **Jeffrey Salkin**

VERSE 2
F G C Am Dm G7
5. Hon - or your par - ents and your life will be long. 6. To mur-der an - oth - er is a
C C7 F G C A7
ter - ri - ble wrong. 7. A mar - riage must be built on trust. 8. Nev - er
Dm7 G7 C
D.C. or continue
steal, be hon - est and just. (9. Don't)
VERSE 3
F G C Am Dm7 G7
lie when you're on the wit - ness stand. 10. Do not de - sire what your
C C7 F G C A7
neigh - bor has. Fol - low these laws that I will give, for
Dm7 G7 C
D.C. al Fine
they will help you live.

The Ten Plagues

Music: **Jeff Klepper**
Text: **Jeff Klepper** and **Jeffrey Salkin**

Originally from the album *Bible People* (ARE) – From the Kol B'Seder album *Songs for Growin'*
To purchase multiple copies for your ensemble, please visit TranscontinentalMusic.com

Am Dm Am G
Dm Gm Dm C
28
your skin, then hail, and lo-custs, so be-ware, oh Phar - aoh,
Em Am
Am Dm
32
D.C.
don't you care?
VERSE 2
Dm Am G Am
Gm Dm C Dm
35
(2.) Mo - ses stretch-ing out his hand will bring to - tal dark-ness to the land, and
Dm Am G Em Am
Gm Dm C Am Dm
39
rit.
slower
then you'll hear all E-gypt cry, for God will make your first-born die. It's
Dm Am G Am Dm
Gm Dm C Dm Gm
44
sad that all this had to be. Peo-ple died so we'd be free. Our drops of wine fall
Am G Em Am
Dm C Am Dm
49
a tempo
D.C. al Fine
down like tears as we re - tell the sto - ry ev - ery year.

This Is Very Good

Music: **Jeff Klepper**
Text: **Chaim Stern**

Originally from the album *Songs NFTY Sings* – From the Kol B'Seder album *Sparks of Torah*
To purchase multiple copies for your ensemble, please visit TranscontinentalMusic.com

994055

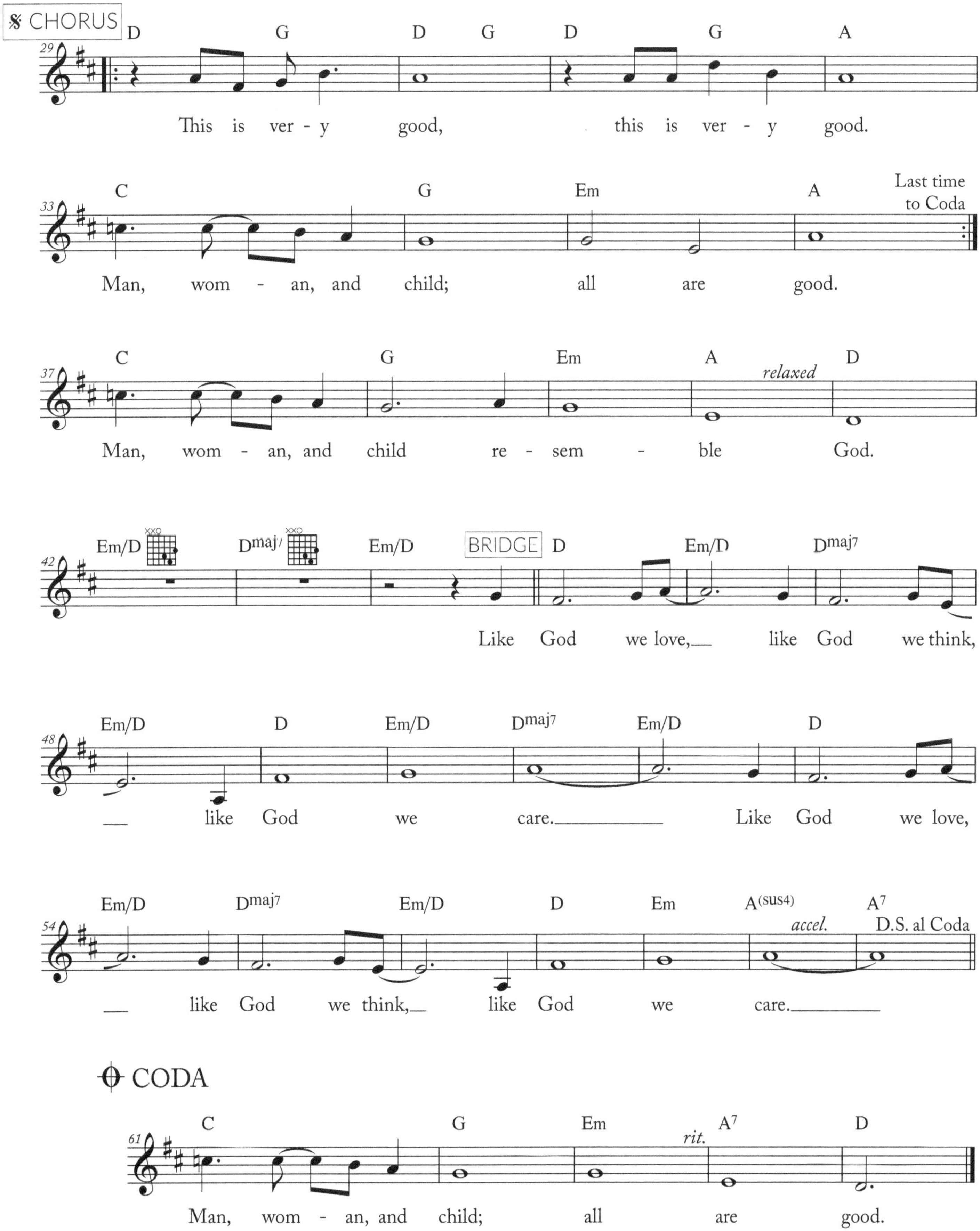
CHORUS
D G D G D G A
This is ver - y good, this is ver - y good.
C G Em A
Last time to Coda
Man, wom - an, and child; all are good.
C G Em A D
relaxed
Man, wom - an, and child re - sem - ble God.
Em/D Dmaj7 Em/D
BRIDGE
D Em/D Dmaj7
Like God we love, like God we think,
Em/D D Em/D Dmaj7 Em/D D
like God we care. Like God we love,
Em/D Dmaj7 Em/D D Em A(sus4) A7
accel.
D.S. al Coda
like God we think, like God we care.
CODA
C G Em A7 D
rit.
Man, wom - an, and child; all are good.

The Torah

עץ חיים היא

Eitz Chayim Hi

Music and English text: **Jeff Klepper**
Hebrew text: Liturgy

Originally from the album *Especially Jewish Symbols* (ARE) – From the Kol B'Seder album *Songs for Growin'*
To purchase multiple copies for your ensemble, please visit TranscontinentalMusic.com

It is a tree of life for those who hold fast to it,
and all its supporters are happy.
Its ways are ways of pleasatness
and all its paths are peace.

עֵץ חַיִּים הִיא לַמַּחֲזִיקִים בָּהּ,
וְתֹמְכֶיהָ מְאֻשָּׁר.
דְּרָכֶיהָ דַרְכֵי נֹעַם,
וְכָל נְתִיבוֹתֶיהָ שָׁלוֹם.

Tov L'hodot

טוב להודות

Music: **Jeff Klepper** and **Dan Freelander**
Text: Psalm 92:2-3

Originally from the album *Songs NFTY Sings* – From the Kol B'Seder album *Snapshots Vol. 1*
To purchase multiple copies for your ensemble, please visit TranscontinentalMusic.com

It is good to praise Adonai;	טוֹב לְהֹדוֹת לַיְיָ
to sing hymns to Your name, O Most High,	וּלְזַמֵּר לְשִׁמְךָ עֶלְיוֹן.
to proclaim Your steadfast love at daybreak,	לְהַגִּיד בַּבֹּקֶר חַסְדֶּךָ,
Your faithfulness each night.	וֶאֱמוּנָתְךָ בַּלֵּילוֹת.

Tzadik Katamar

צדיק כתמר

Music: **Jeff Klepper**
Text: Psalm 92:13-16, 92:5-6

From the album *Yom Chadash*

994055

The righteous bloom like a date-palm;
they thrive like a cedar in Lebanon;
planted in the house of Adonai,
they flourish in the courts of our God.
In old age they still produce fruit;
they are full of sap and freshness,
attesting that Adonai is upright,
my Rock, in whom there is no wrong.
You have gladdened me by Your deeds, Adonai;
I shout for joy at Your handiwork.
How great are Your works, Adonai,
how very subtle Your designs!

צַדִּיק כַּתָּמָר יִפְרָח
כְּאֶרֶז בַּלְּבָנוֹן יִשְׂגֶּה.
שְׁתוּלִים בְּבֵית יְיָ,
בְּחַצְרוֹת אֱלֹהֵינוּ יַפְרִיחוּ.
עוֹד יְנוּבוּן בְּשֵׂיבָה,
דְּשֵׁנִים וְרַעֲנַנִּים יִהְיוּ.
לְהַגִּיד כִּי־יָשָׁר יְיָ,
צוּרִי וְלֹא־עַוְלָתָה בּוֹ.
כִּי שִׂמַּחְתַּנִי יְיָ בְּפָעֳלֶךָ
בְּמַעֲשֵׂי יָדֶיךָ אֲרַנֵּן.
מַה־גָּדְלוּ מַעֲשֶׂיךָ, יְיָ,
מְאֹד עָמְקוּ מַחְשְׁבֹתֶיךָ.

Ushmor

ושמור

Music: **Jeff Klepper** and **Dan Freelander**
Text: Evening liturgy *(Hashkiveinu)*

Originally from the album *Songs NFTY Sings* – From the Kol B'Seder album *Snapshots Vol. 1*
To purchase multiple copies for your ensemble, please visit TranscontinentalMusic.com

Guard our going and coming,	וּשְׁמוֹר צֵאתֵנוּ וּבוֹאֵנוּ,
to life and to peace,	לְחַיִּים וּלְשָׁלוֹם,
evermore.	מֵעַתָּה וְעַד עוֹלָם.
Spread over us the shelter of Your peace.	וּפְרוֹשׂ עָלֵינוּ סֻכַּת שְׁלוֹמֶךָ.

V'ahavta L'rei-acha Kamocha

ואהבת לרעך כמוך

Music: **Jeff Klepper**
Text: Leviticus 19:13, 19:17-18

In memory of Rabbi Robert Samuels

From the album *We Are Partners*
To purchase multiple copies for your ensemble, please visit TranscontinentalMusic.com

Love your fellow neighbor as yourself;
and you shall not defraud your fellow neighbor,
and you shall not hate your kin in your heart.
You shall not take vengeance or bear a grudge.

וְאָהַבְתָּ לְרֵעֲךָ כָּמוֹךָ
וְלֹא־תַעֲשֹׁק אֶת־רֵעֲךָ
וְלֹא־תִשְׂנָא אֶת־אָחִיךָ בִּלְבָבֶךָ.
לֹא־תִקֹּם וְלֹא־תִטֹּר.

V'al Kulam

ועל כלם

Music: **Jeff Klepper**
Text: High Holy Day liturgy

For all these failures of judgment and will, God of forgiveness—
forgive us, pardon us, lead us to atonement.

וְעַל כֻּלָּם, אֱלוֹהַּ סְלִיחוֹת,
סְלַח לָנוּ, מְחַל לָנוּ, כַּפֶּר־לָנוּ.

From the album *We Are Partners*
Also available with piano accompaniment in *Shirei T'shuvah: Songs of Repentance* (TMP 991900).
To purchase multiple copies for your ensemble, please visit TranscontinentalMusic.com

V'eirastich Li וארשתיך לי

Music: **Jeff Klepper** and **Dan Freelander**
Text: Adapted from Hosea 2:21

From the album *In Every Generation*

And I will espouse you forever,
and I will espouse you with righteousness,
and I will espouse you with justice,
and I will espouse you with goodness,
and I will espouse you with mercy,
and I will espouse you with faithfulness,
and I will espouse you forever.

וְאֵרַשְׂתִּיךְ לִי לְעוֹלָם,
וְאֵרַשְׂתִּיךְ לִי בְּצֶדֶק,
וְאֵרַשְׂתִּיךְ בְּמִשְׁפָּט,
וְאֵרַשְׂתִּיךְ בְּחֶסֶד,
וְאֵרַשְׂתִּיךְ בְּרַחֲמִים,
וְאֵרַשְׂתִּיךְ לִי בֶּאֱמוּנָה,
וְאֵרַשְׂתִּיךְ לִי לְעוֹלָם.

V'sham'ru ושמרו

Music: **Jeff Klepper**
Text: Shabbat liturgy

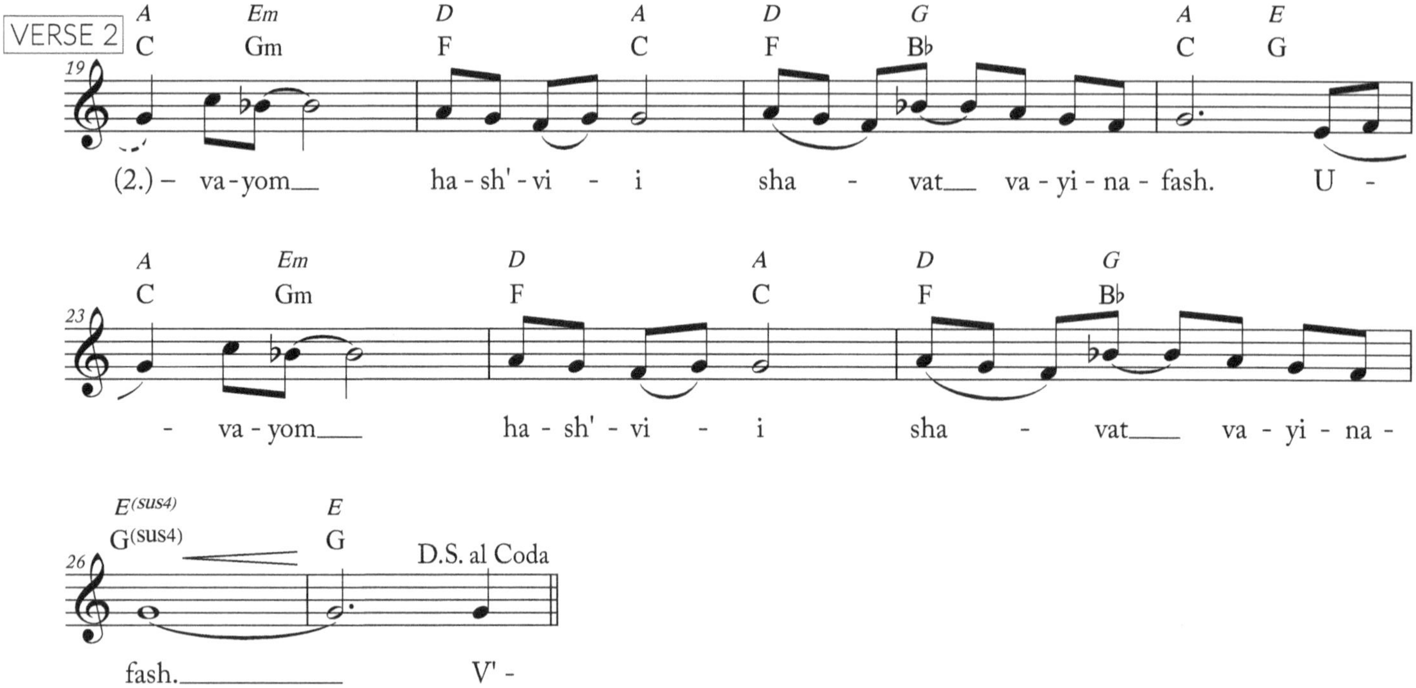

CODA

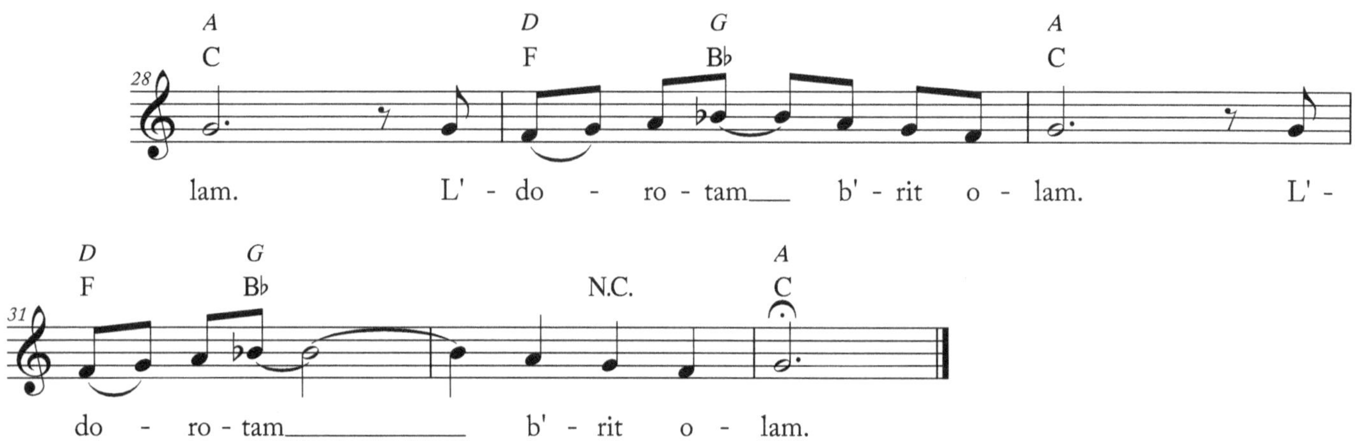

The people of Israel	וְשָׁמְרוּ בְנֵי יִשְׂרָאֵל
shall keep Shabbat,	אֶת־הַשַּׁבָּת,
observing Shabbat throughout the ages	לַעֲשׂוֹת אֶת־הַשַּׁבָּת לְדֹרֹתָם
as a covenant for all time.	בְּרִית עוֹלָם.
It is a sign for all time	בֵּינִי וּבֵין בְּנֵי יִשְׂרָאֵל
between Me and the people of Israel.	אוֹת הִיא לְעֹלָם,
For in six days Adonai made	כִּי־שֵׁשֶׁת יָמִים עָשָׂה יְיָ
heaven and earth,	אֶת־הַשָּׁמַיִם וְאֶת־הָאָרֶץ,
and on the seventh day God ceased from work and was refreshed.	וּבַיּוֹם הַשְּׁבִיעִי שָׁבַת וַיִּנָּפַשׁ.

V'yashvu Ish וישבו איש

Music: **Jeff Klepper** and **Dan Freelander**
Text: Micah 4:4; Isaiah 2:4

Winner of the Bicentennial Song Contest (Jewish Welfare Board, 1976)

Originally from the album *Songs NFTY Sings* – From the Kol B'Seder album *The Bridge*

But every family shall sit under its own vine and fig tree
with no one to disturb them.
Nation shall not take up sword against nation;
they shall never again study war.

וְיָשְׁבוּ אִישׁ תַּחַת גַּפְנוֹ
וְתַחַת תְּאֵנָתוֹ וְאֵין מַחֲרִיד.
לֹא־יִשָּׂא גוֹי אֶל־גּוֹי חֶרֶב,
וְלֹא־יִלְמְדוּ עוֹד מִלְחָמָה.

V'zot HaTorah

וזאת התורה

Music: **Jeff Klepper** and **Dan Freelander**
Text: Torah service

This is the Torah which Moses placed
before the people of Israel,
God's word through the hand of Moses.

וְזֹאת הַתּוֹרָה אֲשֶׁר שָׂם מֹשֶׁה
לִפְנֵי בְּנֵי יִשְׂרָאֵל,
עַל־פִּי יְיָ בְּיַד־מֹשֶׁה.

From the album *Sparks of Torah*
To purchase multiple copies for your ensemble, please visit TranscontinentalMusic.com

We Are Counting

A Song for the Omer

Music and text: **Jeff Klepper**

D C D C
hours, count-ing the days go-ing by, count-ing the days go-ing
D(sus4) D G echo G(sus4) G
by. We are count-ing, one by
D echo 1. D(sus4) D 2. D7 1. continue 2. Fine
one. We are
BRIDGE
G G(sus4) G D D(sus4) D
What is the rea-son, what does it show?
G D F
Where does it lead us, where do we go? How will we get there,
D D(sus4) D F
how will we re-turn? What will we do now
D D.S. al Fine
with what we have learned? If we

We Are Partners

Music and text: **Jeff Klepper**

From the album *We Are Partners*
To purchase multiple copies for your ensemble, please visit TranscontinentalMusic.com

994055

We Remember Them

Music: **Jeff Klepper**
Text: **Sylvan Kamens** and **Jack Riemer**, ad. **Jeff Klepper**

From the album *We Are Partners*

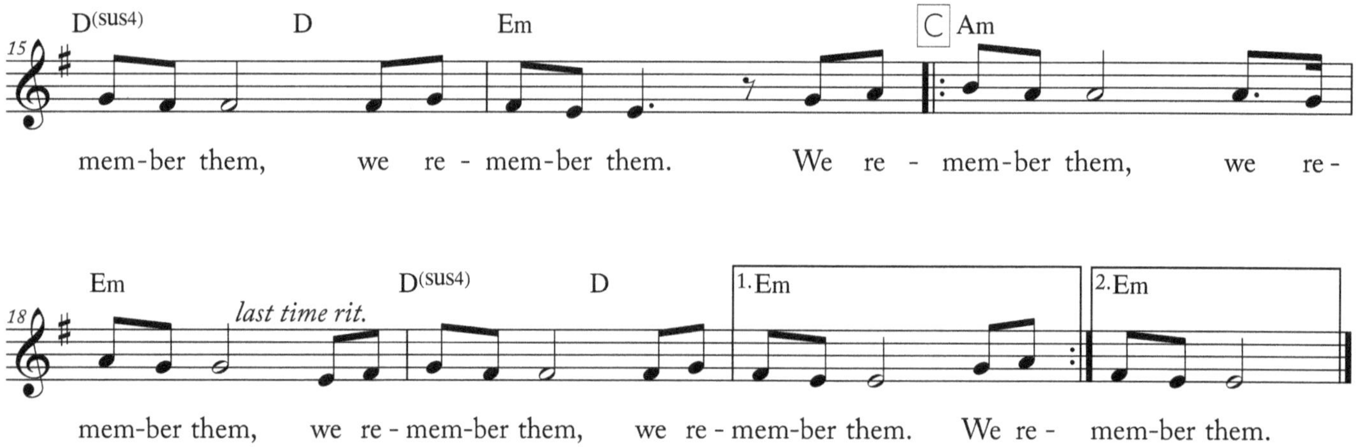
D(sus4) D Em C Am
15
mem-ber them, we re - mem-ber them. We re - mem-ber them, we re -
Em D(sus4) D 1.Em 2.Em
18
last time rit.
mem-ber them, we re - mem-ber them, we re - mem-ber them. We re - mem-ber them.

We Say Shehecheyanu שהחינו

Thank You, God

Music and text: **Jeff Klepper**

Originally from the album *To See the World Through Jewish Eyes Vol. 1* (UAHC) – From the Kol B'Seder album *Songs for Growin'*
To purchase multiple copies for your ensemble, please visit TranscontinentalMusic.com

VERSE 2
C Cmaj7 Dm7 G C E
(2.) times when I learn some-thing new. In our lives there are so man-y things to
Am Am7 Dm7 G7 C Am
do. At the start of ev - ery hol - i - day there is a
F B♭ G(sus4) G
D.S. al Fine
ver - y spe - cial bless-ing that we say. We say, "She -

We Will Be Free

Music and text: **Jeff Klepper** and **Stuart Rosenberg**

Originally from the album *Sing Out for Justice* – From the album *Jeff Klepper Live in Concert*
To purchase multiple copies for your ensemble, please visit TranscontinentalMusic.com

VERSE 2
2. I was for - sa - ken, down as I could be. Then I heard a
mes-sage that set my spir - it free. We can live to - geth-
- er, we will win or lose. And I know that God is watch-
- ing which - ev - er way we choose. We will be
CHORUS 2
free when there is jus - tice. We will be free when there is hope.
We will be free when we join to - geth - er. We will be
free, yes, we will be free. And if there's dark-

BRIDGE
Bm G D
53
- ness deep in - side you, and it's hold - ing on so
A Bm A
56
strong, there's a light that's al - ways shin - - ing, it's been shin-
G A
60
- ing for so long. We will be
CHORUS 3
G A D G A
63
free when there's no hun - ger. We will be free when there is no pain.
D G A Bm
66
We will be free when we love each oth - er. We will be
C 1. A
69
free, yes, we will be free. We will be
2. A
73
free.

With My Family

Music and English text: **Jeff Klepper**
Hebrew text: Traditional

Originally from the album *To See the World Through Jewish Eyes Vol. 1* (UAHC) – From the Kol B'Seder album *Songs for Growin'*
To purchase multiple copies for your ensemble, please visit TranscontinentalMusic.com

VERSE 2 (CHANUKAH)
(2.) Cha - nu - kah to - geth-er a - round the shin-ing lights, with games and songs and
pres-ents ev - ery night.
slightly faster
"Ma - oz tzur y' - shu - a - ti l' -
cha na - eh l' - sha - bei - ach."
a tempo
Cha-nu-kah is a ver - y spe-cial
time,
Cha - nu - kah is a fam - i - ly time.
It
D.S.
VERSE 3 (PASSOVER)
(3.) at our Pe - sach se - der we gath - er ev - ery year, wait - ing for E -
li - jah to ap-pear.
slightly faster
"Da, da - yei - nu, da, da - yei - nu,
da, da - yei - nu, da - yei - nu, da - yei - nu."
a tempo
Pe-sach is a ver - y spe-cial
time,
Pe - sach is a fam - i - ly time.
It
D.S. al Fine

Who brings forth bread from the earth...	הַמּוֹצִיא לֶחֶם מִן הָאָרֶץ...
Rock of Ages let our song praise Your saving power.	מָעוֹז צוּר יְשׁוּעָתִי, לְךָ נָאֶה לְשַׁבֵּחַ.
It would have been enough.	דַּיֵּנוּ.

Yeish Kochavim

יש כוכבים

There Are Stars

Music: **Jeff Klepper**
Text: **Hannah Senesh**, English adaptation by **Jeff Klepper** and **Dan Freelander**

Originally from the album *Yom Chadash* – From the Kol B'Seder album *In Every Generation*
Also available in separate edition for SAB choir and keyboard (TMP 993115).
To purchase multiple copies for your ensemble, please visit TranscontinentalMusic.com

A D E C A Amaj7 D E
de - rech, There are stars up a - bove, so far a - way we on - ly see their
F♯m C♯m Bm E A E
light long long af - ter the star it - self is gone. And so it is with
F♯m D Bm E
peo - ple that we loved. Their mem - o - ries keep shin - ing, ev - er
D Bm E(sus4) E
bright - ly, though their time with us is done. But the
C♯m F♯m F F♯m F
stars that light up the dark - est night, these are the lights that
E(sus4) E D A E D A
guide us. As we live our days these are the ways we re - mem -
Bm E(sus4) E A E
- ber, we re - mem - ber. As we live our days these
D A Bm E A D E
D.S. al Coda
are the ways we re - mem - ber, we re - mem - ber.

𝄌 CODA

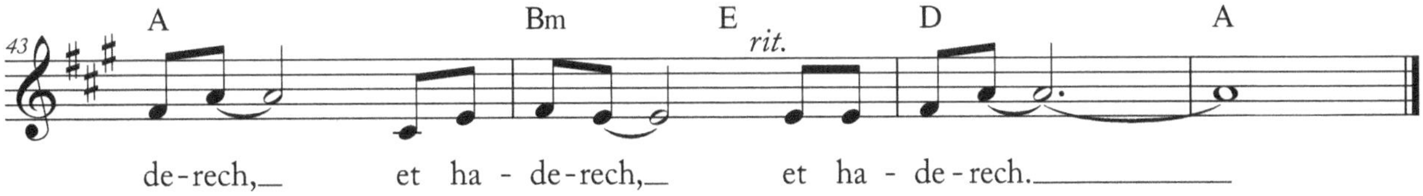

There are stars up above, so far away we only see their light
long, long after the star itself is gone.
And so it is with people that we loved—
their memories keep shining ever brightly
though their time with us is done.
But the stars that light up the darkest night,
these are the lights that guide us.
As we live our days, these are the ways we remember.

יֵשׁ כּוֹכָבִים שֶׁאוֹרָם מַגִּיעַ אַרְצָה
רַק כַּאֲשֶׁר הֵם עַצְמָם אָבְדוּ וְאֵינָם.
יֵשׁ אֲנָשִׁים שֶׁזִּיו זִכְרָם מֵאִיר
כַּאֲשֶׁר הֵם עַצְמָם
אֵינָם עוֹד בְּתוֹכֵנוּ.
אוֹרוֹת אֵלֶּה הַמַּבְהִיקִים
בְּחֶשְׁכַת הַלַּיִל.
הֵם הֵם שֶׁמַּרְאִים לָאָדָם אֶת הַדֶּרֶךְ.

Yism'chu ישמחו

Music: **Jeff Klepper**
Text: Shabbat liturgy

From the album *The Bridge*
Choral and accompanied versions available on TranscontinentalMusic.com
To purchase multiple copies for your ensemble, please visit TranscontinentalMusic.com

Those who keep Shabbat by calling it a delight
will rejoice in Your realm.
The people that hallows Shabbat
will delight in Your goodness.
For, being pleased with the Seventh Day,
You hallowed it as the most precious of days,
drawing our attention to the work of Creation.

יִשְׂמְחוּ בְמַלְכוּתְךָ
שׁוֹמְרֵי שַׁבָּת וְקוֹרְאֵי עֹנֶג.
עַם מְקַדְּשֵׁי שְׁבִיעִי,
כֻּלָּם יִשְׂבְּעוּ וְיִתְעַנְּגוּ מִטּוּבֶךָ.
וְהַשְּׁבִיעִי רָצִיתָ בּוֹ וְקִדַּשְׁתּוֹ,
חֶמְדַּת יָמִים אוֹתוֹ קָרָאתָ,
זֵכֶר לְמַעֲשֵׂה בְרֵאשִׁית.

Yom Chadash

יום חדש

Shir Yahel

שיר יהל

Music: **Jeff Klepper**
Text: **Gidon Elad**

 994055

בּוֹא נָשִׁיר עַל יוֹם חָדָשׁ בַּעֲרָבָה,
יוֹם יָהֵל אוֹרוֹת מְלוֹא יָדֵינוּ.
בּוֹא נָשִׁיר עַל טִיפְּטִיפּוֹנֶת אַהֲבָה,
שֶׁהִכְּתָה, הִכְּתָה קוֹל מֵיתָרֵינוּ.

Let's sing of a new day in the Aravah,
Yahel's day, our hands full of light.
Let's sing of a little bit of love,
That struck a chord on our strings.

יוֹם חָדָשׁ, כִּנּוֹר נוֹגֵן בַּסֶּלַע.
יוֹם חָדָשׁ, יֵשׁ פֶּרַח בַּחוֹלוֹת.
יוֹם חָדָשׁ, עֲצֵי תָּמָר לְפֶלֶא.
יוֹם חָדָשׁ, חַיִּים מֵחֲלוֹמוֹת.

A new day, a rock plays the harp's melody.
A new day, there's a flower in the sand.
A new day, magnificent palm trees.
A new day, life from dreams.

בּוֹא נִצְחַק אֶת חוֹם הַקַּיִץ הַלּוֹהֵט,
חוֹם יָהֵל זֵעָה מְלוֹא גּוּפֵנוּ.
בּוֹא נִצְחַק עִם הַצּוּקִים וְהַלֵּילוֹת,
אֶת הָאָבִיב הַטּוֹב, אָבִיב חַיֵּינוּ.

Let's laugh with the summer's radiating heat,
Yahel's heat of sweat-covered bodies.
Let's laugh along with the mountain peaks and the night,
The good springtime, the springtime of our lives.

Yotzeir Or

יוצר אור

Music: **Jeff Klepper**
Text: Morning liturgy

Praised are You,
Adonai our God, Sovereign of the universe,
Creator of light and darkness,
who makes peace and fashions all things.

בָּרוּךְ אַתָּה, יְיָ,
אֱלֹהֵינוּ מֶלֶךְ הָעוֹלָם,
יוֹצֵר אוֹר וּבוֹרֵא חֹשֶׁךְ,
עֹשֶׂה שָׁלוֹם וּבוֹרֵא אֶת־הַכֹּל.

994055

You Are Stormwind

Music: **Jeff Klepper**
Text: **Chaim Stern**

From the album *The Bridge* – Alternate version on *In This Place*
To purchase multiple copies for your ensemble, please visit TranscontinentalMusic.com

C
meno mosso
Em Em6(add9) Em7 Em6(add9) Em Em6(add9) Em7 Em6(add9) Am7
dark- ness, You are com - fort, You are,
Bm7 Em Em6(add9) Em7 Em6(add9) Em Em6(add9)
You are my light. You are win - ter,
Em7 Em6(add9) Em Em6(add9) Em7 Em6(add9) Am7
You are shel - ter, You are my
F♯m B7 Em Em6(add9) Em7 Em6(add9)
heart.
D
Cmaj7 Am7 Bm Em Cmaj7 Am7 Bm Em
Now at last I've found You, now at last I am found,
Cmaj7 Am7 Bm Em Cmaj7 Am7 Bm Em Cmaj7 Am7 Bm Em
now at last I've found You, now at last I am found, now at last I've found You,
Cmaj7 Am7 Bm Am7 F♯m B7 Em
rit.
now at last I am found, I am found.

You Can Change the World

Music and text: **Jeff Klepper** and **Donald Rossoff**

Originally from the album *To See the World through Jewish Eyes Vol. 2* (UAHC) – From the Kol B'Seder album *Songs for Growin'*
To purchase multiple copies for your ensemble, please visit TranscontinentalMusic.com

CHORUS
G C G Em G Em Am7 D7
you can change the world. You can make the world com - plete.
C G B7 Em C D
Take the pride you feel in - side and nev - er ac - cept de - feat.
1.2. G D 3. G
2. "There's an
3. So

Y'varech'cha

יברכך

Priestly Blessing

Music: **Jeff Klepper** and **Dan Freelander**
Text: Numbers 6:24-26

From the album *Sparks of Torah*
To purchase multiple copies for your ensemble, please visit TranscontinentalMusic.com

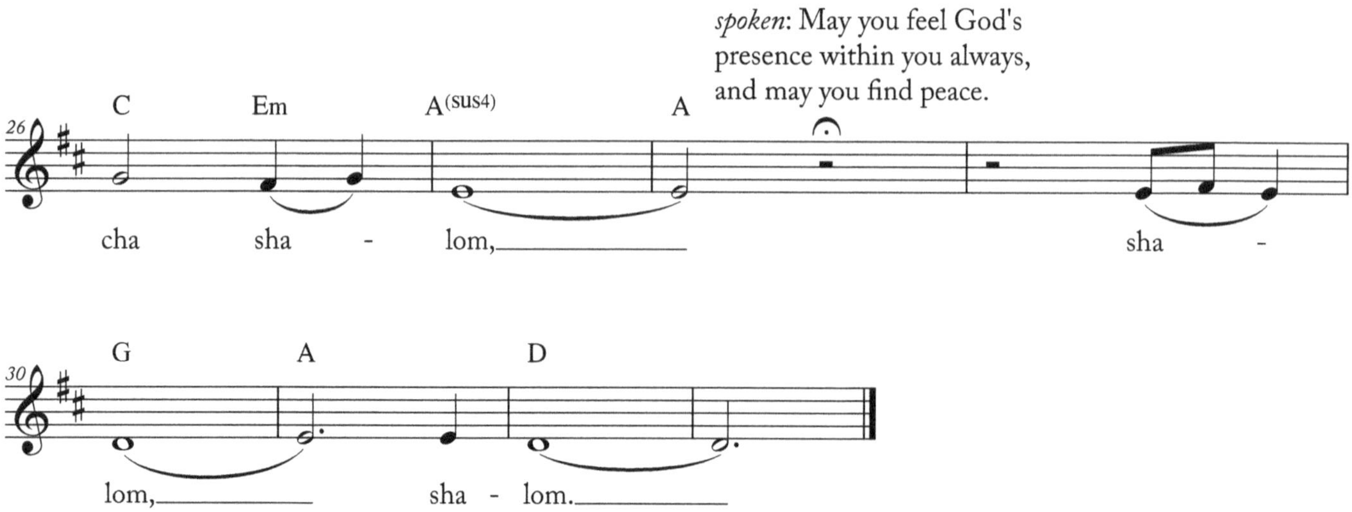

May God bless you and keep you.
May God's light shine upon you, and may God be gracious to you.
My you feel God's presence within you always,
and may you find peace.

יְבָרֶכְךָ יְיָ וְיִשְׁמְרֶךָ.
יָאֵר יְיָ פָּנָיו אֵלֶיךָ וִיחֻנֶּךָּ.
יִשָּׂא יְיָ פָּנָיו אֵלֶיךָ
וְיָשֵׂם לְךָ שָׁלוֹם.

Zeh Hayom

זה-היום

Music: **Jeff Klepper**
Text: Psalm 118:24

Composed for the Rashi School Dedication (Dedham, Massachusetts), September, 2010

From the album *We Are Partners*

This is the day that Adonai has made—
let us exult and rejoice on it.

זֶה־הַיּוֹם עָשָׂה יְיָ
נָגִילָה וְנִשְׂמְחָה בוֹ.

The Songs of Kol B'Seder

Abraham In June of 1972, Danny and I drove from Worcester, Massachusetts, to Colorado Springs to participate in the Rocky Mountain Curriculum Planning Workshop, where college-age teachers came together to study, dream, and brainstorm new ideas for Jewish religious schools. We soon realized that music had the potential to transform Jewish education by bringing the spirit of camp into the Jewish classroom, where enjoyable songs could be used to teach concepts and values while strengthening Jewish identity. Audrey Friedman Marcus, co-founder of the workshop we attended, asked me to compose a series of new songs for religious school use, many of which are included here, including "Abraham." (JK)

Adon Olam There are two well-known melodies for "Adon Olam." One is by the nineteenth-century Ukrainian cantor Eliezer Gerovitch (in minor), while the composer of the other (in major), the one beloved by children that sounds like a military march, is unknown. Such has been the fate of "Adon Olam," the *piyut* whose profound theological themes get lost when paired with trivial tunes. (Even more questionable is the tendency of some congregations to sing these words to the latest pop hit.) That said, my humble addition to the "Adon Olam" collection, though hardly meant to be the definitive version, is an uptempo setting, heavily influenced by the Brazilian style that was popular in Israel in the 1980s. (JK)

Adonai, Adonai It was the summer of 2022 and Danny was approaching his seventieth birthday. I don't write that many songs these days, but this occasion clearly called for one, so I asked his wife, Elyse (who is a rabbi), to recommend a text, and without hesitation this is what she suggested. Not only are these words from Exodus so vital in our liturgy, they are a reminder of the responsibility to "imitate" God's love for humanity in order to become our best selves. (JK)

Adonai Oz (Y'vareich et Amo) This anthem reminds us that we need strength to achieve peace. Our setting starts out by asserting that our communal strength is one of God's greatest blessings to our people and then asks God to also bless us with peace. This timeless message (and its inherent opportunities for communal singing and harmonies) makes it one of our favorite closing songs. (DF)

Af, Peh, Ozen The 1970s was a time of tremendous change in Jewish education. A new generation of baby boomers, now teaching in religious schools across the country, quickly found that textbooks and lesson plans from prior generations were hopelessly out of date. Jewish education became a top priority, which led to the formation of CAJE (Coalition for Alternatives in Jewish Education) and the creation of mountains of new curricula. Debbie Friedman's "Alef Bet" comes from this period, as do several songs included here: "Af Peh Ozen," "We Say Shehecheyanu," and "With My Family," all written for the Reform Movement's 1980s curriculum, *To See the World Through Jewish Eyes*. (JK)

Again and Again Rabbi Chaim Stern had the rare ability to distill the essential meanings of a prayer into a few lines of graceful poetry. In his festival siddur for young children, *Gates of Joy*, he included these lines as a commentary on the prayer *Avot V'Imahot*. I could not resist setting a simple, joyful melody to the Zen-like verse "Again and again, today and today, again and again and today." (JK)

Ahavah Rabbah This meditative chant takes its words from the morning liturgy, but it was not composed as a worship melody. The tune came to me when I was suddenly confronted with vocal problems toward the end of the 1990s, a vexing situation that had no immediate resolution. In addition to seeking medical advice, I began a daily meditation practice. During my meditation sessions, words and phrases from Hebrew prayers would often echo in my mind, sometimes with a melody, and I used them as my mantra. "Ahavah Rabbah" was one of those phrases. I encourage you to listen to the recording with your eyes closed and let the music wash over you. (JK)

Al Sh'loshah D'varim I (HaOlam Omeid) This energetic rock version of the well-known verse from *Pirkei Avot* is as different from the popular Chassidic Festival melody as could be. Throughout the 1970s and '80s, the new music that we and others were creating was predominately in a folk style. Our songs were relatively simple, easy to sing, and usually played on guitar. While the new sounds we were creating were not to everyone's taste, our music was *heimish* and accessible. The genre we now call "Jewish Rock" had not yet crystallized, which makes this song (especially the recording) something of an outlier in our catalog. (JK)

Al Sh'loshah D'varim II (HaOlam Kayam) Here's an instant lesson for all the teachers out there: Compare two or more contrasting versions of "Al Sh'loshah" from our sacred texts. So many questions arise. What do the Hebrew words mean? Why the number three? Can *d'varim* mean more than just "things"? What would you select for your own top-three list? For this text, one of the lesser known variations of the "Al Sh'loshah" formulation (included in the *Gates of Prayer* Torah service), I wrote a simple melody to sing while opening the ark to take out the Torah. (JK)

Aleinu It takes chutzpah to say, "Hey, Jewish people, I have a better way for you to sing this prayer. I know you've been singing it one way since you were a small child, but I think you'll like this new one if you give it a chance." When cantors teach prayers to children, we say, "That's our tradition. We've been singing it this way for generations!" Clearly, this "Aleinu" melody is not going to suddenly become traditional. But over time, we do tend to choose melodies that say something about ourselves and the world we inhabit. Let's also remember: Every traditional tune, once upon a time, was brand-new, just like this one. (JK)

Anah Halach Dodeich *Shir HaShirim* (Song of Songs), one of the five *m'gillot*, has long been the textual source of a beloved genre of Israeli popular music, giving us classics such as "Dodi Li," "Iti Milvanon," "El Ginat Egoz," and so many others. Following a tradition to read from *Shir HaShirim* on Friday afternoon (as well as Pesach), these were among the songs we would sing to welcome Shabbat at camp in the 1970s. Several years later, working at the Leo Baeck High School in Haifa and singing those same songs with Israeli teens every Friday evening, I was moved to recapture the feeling of those classic songs for myself. "Anah Halach Dodeich" (in addition to "Hanitzanim" and "K'shoshanah") is the result. (JK)

Another Year, Another Chanukah How many insipid token Chanukah songs must we endure at elementary and middle school holiday choral concerts? This is our attempt to bring a simple, honest statement about our favorite winter holiday with an easy sing-along chorus. Share it with your public school music teachers! (DF)

Ashrei The title of one of our earliest songs, "Ashrei," means "joy and gladness." This upbeat setting from Psalms 84 and 144 is guaranteed to get your students clapping and singing along and is a perfect opening song for *Minchah* services. (DF)

Ashrei Adam Matza Chochmah This text from Proverbs opened one of the Torah services in *Gates of Prayer*. Our upbeat melody celebrates our search for wisdom (*chochmah*) and understanding, for the fruits of our study of Torah are better than "money, silver, or gold." (DF)

Ashreinu Written during my cantorial school years, this was one of the first minor key songs I composed. Prior to that, I thought that writing in major sounded more "American." Perhaps I had been trying to avoid writing songs that sounded like the Yiddish tunes of my grandparents or the Israeli Chassidic Song Festival songs that were coming out of Israel at the time. But the more I studied Jewish music, the more I realized that major and minor chords (and other musical modes we won't get into here) can be seen as distinctive flavors. Just as in cooking, they need to be carefully balanced. (JK)

Avinu Malkeinu Like many, I love the "traditional" tunes we grew up singing, and there is no better example than the melody for "Avinu Malkeinu." No one seems to know where that tune originated or how long we have been singing it. This "Avinu Malkeinu," like several other songs here, was composed for my senior recital at HUC-JIR in 1980, a contemporary musical service for *S'lichot*. (See "Hashkiveinu.") In 1980 I was twenty-six, hardly an age of sophistication, but I was still keenly aware that the music created to accompany our worship must be relatable and accessible. While this setting incorporates a familiar folk-rock style, the minor-key melody accentuates suspended and discordant notes to express our pleading with God, in the tradition of the famous Chasidic rebbe Levi Yitzchak of Berditchev. (JK)

Baruch She-amar I love this prayer from the morning liturgy, which introduces a selection of psalms called *P'sukei D'zimrah*. For many years I chanted the paragraph according to *nusach*, the traditional prayer mode, even as I searched for a usable tune, but nothing caught my ear. I finally realized that I could do both—sing and chant—at the same time and composed this simple melody. I introduced it at my daughter Liora's bat mitzvah in 2006 and have sung it every Shabbat morning since. (JK)

Bayom Hahu The so-called traditional "Bayom Hahu" melody is attributed to Brooklyn Rabbi Israel Goldfarb, which would make it around a hundred years old, though you might think it much older by its near universal use. Some disparage the tune, comparing it to "The Farmer in the Dell" (while its companion piece, "Shehu Noteh Shamayim," also written by Goldfarb, is often derided as "The Itsy Bitsy Spider"). This is unfair. The melodies themselves do exactly what they were designed for: They enable the congregation to sing together. But what happens when the worship leader wants to introduce a different tune? I composed this melody in Israel and came to like it so much that I decided to replace the old tune with this one, singing it with my congregation each week for two decades, and to my surprise and delight, no one ever complained. (JK)

The Bimah Song To a young child, there is something magical about the bimah and its symbols. I can't remember who came up with the line "I'd rather be on the bimah than sitting in my chair" (it may have been my co-lyricist, Rabbi Susan Nanus), but the line perfectly captures the sense of wonderment children have when they sit in the sanctuary for the first time. Written for Alternatives in Religious Education (ARE) in the mid-1970s, it helped establish the warm and whimsical tone that many of my later religious school songs would adopt. (JK)

B'sefer Chayim For me, every song begins with a text. Something calls out, a rhyme, a catchy rhythm, an alliteration, or perhaps a powerful message that yearns to be expressed. When I sit down with guitar, notebook, pencil, and recorder, that's when the painstaking work of piecing notes and chords together like a jigsaw puzzle begins. There are many liturgical texts—and here is an example of one—that resist being turned into an ordinary song. Look at the first measure and you can see that I was clearly thinking about "Shalom Rav," the prayer that incorporates it on the *Yamim Noraim* (High Holy Days). But the text leads the way. In this case it forced me to go in a different direction, which is why this particular setting ended up as a blend of folk, art song, and davening (prayer chanting). (JK)

Chanukah Lights The most effective children's songs teach one basic concept in an enjoyable and memorable way. The point here was to teach not about Chanukah per se, but about the light of (what in Israel is called) the *chanukiyah*, along with the tradition of displaying the lights in our windows. (JK)

Chatzi Kaddish I love composing new liturgical melodies immediately following a service, when I am filled with a sense of inner peace and the words of the siddur are still tumbling around my brain. On one occasion I returned home after *Kabbalat Shabbat*, grabbed my guitar, opened the siddur, and this melody came pouring out. Was I unwittingly influenced by Nurit Hirsch's "Bashanah Habaah"? Quite possibly. (JK)

Chazak, Chazak A good example of how we borrow from other cultures is our interest in spirituality and Eastern religions, which manifested itself in the late twentieth century as a new kind of Jewish song influenced by styles as disparate as Chasidic *nigunim*, Native American chant, and African drumming. Many of these simple Judaic chants were incorporated into new Jewish healing rituals. In "Chazak, Chazak," the words we sing to conclude the public reading of each book of Torah, are reimagined as a prayer for personal and communal healing. (JK)

Coming Home The ingathering of Jews from every corner of the world is the cornerstone of any teaching about Israel. The *aliyah* of Jews from hundreds of communities and cultures continues to inspire and clarify the importance of a land and home for our people. The folk-country refrain may sound American, but the message is pure Zionism. (DF)

Cowboy Jew from Mars Writers have silly things pop into our heads all the time, but usually we have the good sense to ignore them. Not this time. I couldn't resist the rhyme of "Mars" and "candy bars." Had I been listening to a little too much of the late Kinky Friedman? But seriously, embedded beneath this bit of silliness is a paean to Jewish food culture, from kashrut to bagels and lox, with a few choice Yiddishisms thrown in for good measure. (JK)

Eichah Ashir When Danny and I began our songwriting partnership some fifty years ago, we wanted our music to sound unique, and we enjoyed the challenge of searching for interesting texts, experimenting with chords and rhythms that went beyond the usual. Here is the result of an evening's work that we put aside to finish later, but never got back to. It has never been heard, until its inclusion in this book and accompanying recording. (JK)

Eilu D'varim During and after my year living in Israel (1981–82), influenced by songwriters such as David Broza, I began to use more minor keys and Israeli rhythms in my songs. I had wanted to use this text in worship, but none of the versions I knew could be easily sung by the congregation, so I wrote my own. (JK)

Elohim Y'choneinu (Psalm 67) The first part of this simple chant can be sung as a catch (a type of canon) with multiple parts joining every measure or two until the room is echoing with voices. This text from Psalm 67, expressing God's blessing of the world, with words reminiscent of the Priestly Blessing, is often read during *S'firat HaOmer* and other sacred occasions, but the prayerful verses are appropriate anytime. (JK)

Empty Chair I am grateful to Rabbi Lawrence Kushner for his teaching on the mystical meaning of the prophet Elijah and explaining the connection between Elijah's chair and the throne of Rabbi Nachman of Bratzlav. This particular song is a good example of how music can be used to teach big ideas, as well as being appropriate for occasions such as Pesach and *Havdalah*. (JK)

Esa Einai The famous version by Shlomo Carlebach was one of the first songs I learned at camp. Composing a text that already has a well-known melody can be challenging. My usual approach in those situations is to start with the opposite of what has already been done. Change minor to major, fast to slow, and so on. In this case, I kept the song in minor but slowed it down for a more prayerful feeling. There is a noticeable Israeli influence here, with a feel similar to other songs of mine such as "Anah Halach Dodeich" and "Hashiveinu." (JK)

Give Me Sleep (Hashkiveinu) In the note for "You Are Stormwind" I talk about my introduction to the liturgical poetry of Rabbi Chaim Stern, with whom I served as cantor for two years. The metrical lines of "Stormwind" were relatively straightforward to set, but the free verse of "Give Me Sleep" was more challenging, as each section required a slightly different melodic and harmonic approach. As I got deeper into the text, I found myself constructing a melodic suite with the opening phrase serving as a primary theme. While I wouldn't exactly call the result "jazz," I was excited to be able to stretch beyond the rigidity of the pop-song format. (JK)

Halomeid One of the most abundant sources of song texts from our tradition is *Pirkei Avot*. This unique tractate of the Talmud is filled with wisdom, philosophy, logic, humor, and good old common sense. Some years ago I wanted to help honor a leader of my congregation who had excelled in Torah study, so I wrote this song for him. "One who teaches even a single letter to another is worthy of praise." What a beautiful teaching. (JK)

Haneirot Halalu Here's a little secret. Many of the texts I have set to music were written for a simple reason: I didn't know any other tune. There are certainly other melodies for "Haneirot Halalu," but I never learned them, and the ones I found in books didn't appeal to me. Because I wrote this in Israel, the influence of Israeli folk song is obvious. Also, I have added the *imahot* (mothers) along with *avot* (fathers) and provided the option of following the Israeli Reform siddur's version, which substitutes *nechamot* (consolations) for the traditional wording, *milchamot* (wars). (JK)

Hanitzanim I have written elsewhere (see "Anah Halach Dodeich") about the beautiful tradition of welcoming Shabbat with songs from *Shir HaShirim* (Song of Songs). Before living in Israel, I could not have imagined how meaningful it would be to compose songs for biblical verses not far from where they were first written thousands of years ago. I could hear in my mind the lilt of shepherds' flutes and feel the tapping of a *tof* in my heart as I channeled the music of the land. (JK)

Haporeis Sukkat Shalom Another of my Haifa songs, the tune of "Haporeis" betrays its influence. In 1979, James Taylor's cover of the Goffin-King classic "Up On the Roof" was a huge hit. Sitting in my Haifa apartment two years later, this "Hashkiveinu" blessing caught my eye, so I sat down with my guitar and a tape recorder to compose. Playing a D major chord, my fingers and brain must have channeled Carole King's melody and James Taylor's guitar style. Of all my songs written in Israel, this is the most American sounding. One element that sticks out is the word repetition of *atah* and *shalom*, giving the lyric a rhythmic groove that propels it forward. Back in the States I didn't think much of the song until my friend, jazz musician Howard Levy, changed one or two chords and suggested slowing it down. Since then it has become one of my personal favorites. (JK)

Hashiveinu In 1980, the CCAR published the Reform Movement's first *S'lichot* service. I decided to compose new music for *S'lichot* for my senior recital at HUC-JIR and called it a "jazz service," with the idea that instrumental improvisation would be a strong element along with melodies sung by the congregation. Jazz saxophonist Arnie Lawrence accompanied me and brought the music to life. The new and untraditional sounds engendered controversy among the HUC-JIR faculty, as it also did, several years later, when shared with my congregation. While "Hashiveinu" was the first of the group to be published, several of the new tunes became a traditional part of my *S'lichot* services for the rest of my career. (JK)

Healing Prayer (Adonai Y'vareich) Throughout history, people have sought to use prayer to heal maladies, physical ailments, and emotional conditions. Traditional versions of the prayer "Mi Shebeirach" (the One who blesses) address these varied concerns. In 1945, Rabbi Mordecai Kaplan published the first modern "Mi Shebeirach," asking God not only to heal the afflicted, but to bless the efforts of human doctors and healers. It is from Kaplan's prayer that these Hebrew lines originate, to which I added a singable translation in English. (When I use this version in synagogue, I usually sing only the Hebrew or English, omitting many of the empty measures.) (JK)

Hineih Mah Tov Blues The song "Hineih Mah Tov" (the slow one that most everybody knows, though its author is unknown) is the first Hebrew folk song that I remember learning. This particular version is notable for being the fastest tune I ever wrote. I was visiting a synagogue one Sunday morning, singing with each religious school class in the sanctuary, when, during a short break, I thought it might be fun to create a new song on the spot. Its form is the classic "call and response," and while it took only a few minutes to write, it's still lots of fun to sing. (JK)

Hodo al Eretz A few years ago, I was looking through a box of cassette tapes and found this forgotten song that Danny and I had written years earlier. Its style is reminiscent of Israeli Chassidic Song Festival tunes such as "Al Sh'loshah D'varim" (by Chaim Tzur), but the text appears only once in the siddur, while returning the Torah scroll to the ark. I liked the tune, and I couldn't understand why we had neglected it. I can only guess that its limited usefulness led us to pay more attention to other songs, while this one sat patiently in a shoebox waiting to be rediscovered. (JK)

Hold Fast to Dreams (The Bridge) Rabbi Chaim Stern published a prayer book for children called *Gates of Joy* that placed two very different poems together on one page. The first, titled "The Bridge," was a little known verse in Yiddish by the early twentieth-century poet Yehoash, the pen name of Solomon Blumgarten. The second was Langston Hughes's famous poem from the Harlem Renaissance, "Hold Fast to Dreams." Reaching for my guitar, I could feel the words leaping off the page, and the melody came easily. These two poems emerged from vastly different worlds, yet both are tender expressions of yearning and hope. (JK)

I Will Plant for My Children (Honi's Song) When I was young, my grandparents kept a blue and white tzedakah box in the kitchen emblazoned with the letters JNF. The Jewish National Fund used those coins to plant millions of trees in Israel. In religious school we would buy little stamps to stick on a page, hoping to collect enough stamps to plant our very own tree. For those of us living in northern climes, the fifteenth of Sh'vat, Tu BiShvat (the new year of the trees), often occurs in January, when all you see out the window is snow. That's where Honi comes in. This mysterious man from Talmudic times who drew magic circles on the ground is as captivating a figure to children as Johnny Appleseed or Rip Van Winkle, and his lesson for us may be more important today than ever. (JK)

Ilu Finu I have always loved this text from the siddur. So many of our prayers remind us of our responsibility to take care of the natural world, to live in harmony with nature, and to see the work of our Creator in every living thing. Yet this passage is uniquely powerful in the way it places us at the shore of the sea, the source of natural life, calling us to lift our voices in thanks toward the heavens, higher than the eagle flies. Listen carefully and you will hear echoes of the Torah blessing melody in the verse. (JK)

Im Ein Ani Li Danny's middle name is Hillel, and these words of Rabbi Hillel hold special meaning for us. Indeed, this *Pirkei Avot* text is considered by some to be the most important teaching in our tradition. Since its coinage, some two thousand years ago, every generation of Jews has sought to understand their place in the world through the prism of Hillel's Talmudic dictum. For our third album, *In Every Generation*, we asked Cantor Riki Lippitz to add her harmony to ours. Her musical gifts, together with the amazing harmonica playing of Howard Levy, contributed to create one of the most exciting recordings in our catalog. (JK)

I'm Growin' Roughly speaking, there are two kinds of religious school songs: Those that teach and those that inspire. This is an example of the latter. Its purpose is to instill Jewish identity and pride in our youngest students. Initially composed for the UAHC's 1980s curriculum *To See the World Through Jewish Eyes*, we chose this as the theme for our own children's song collection, *Songs for Growin'*. (JK)

In Every Generation (B'chol Dor Vador) This central text of the Pesach Haggadah is such a radical statement. We must understand that we are the twenty-first century incarnations of those slaves who came out of Egypt. In every generation, we struggle to escape the metaphorical Egypt that enslaves our minds and the contemporary equivalent societies that enslave their citizens. The message of memory applies to us as individuals, to us as a community, and to every place where people yearn to be free. (DF)

In the Beginning Can you recite the order of Creation without peeking at Genesis 1? Music is the ultimate memory aid (which is how my daughters taught themselves the names of the fifty states and all the US presidents: by singing along with *Schoolhouse Rock* on television!). This song, along with others on our *Songs for Growin'* album, is a fun way to learn basic Jewish knowledge that will be lodged in our memory for a very long time. (JK)

In This Place During a synagogue job interview many years ago, the rabbi asked me if there was a biblical figure with whom I identified. "Jacob!" I said, not missing a beat. I explained that I identified with the rebellious spirit of the young "Yaakov," yet also admired his later transformation into the God-wrestling "Yisrael." While I didn't get the job, I did get a song out of it, thanks to the title of a book by one of my teachers, Rabbi Lawrence Kushner, *God Was in This Place and I, I Did Not Know* (Jewish Lights). The song begins in the Torah and ends up in the here and now; it's also one of my most personal songs. (JK)

Jeff's Nigun Wordless melodies—*nigunim*—hold a special place in the world of Jewish music. Some *nigunim* are introspective and quiet, like a single drop of water, while others can barely be contained, exploding with the power of a cascading waterfall. "Jeff's Nigun" was composed during a plane flight, in my head, which is why it's very simple, but it is a nice way to begin a song session or worship service, to get people singing together easily. (JK)

Jonah This was a fun song to write, with much appreciation to my co-writer, Rabbi Jeff Salkin. I have gotten a little grief for referring in the song to a whale rather than a big fish swallowing Jonah, all in service of a rhyme. That's fair. This story, and the song it inspired, is about taking responsibility for our actions and the fruitlessness of running away from God, a lesson for all, especially on Yom Kippur. (JK)

Ki Anu Amecha This was composed for my senior recital at HUC-JIR (see "Hashiveinu"). I had begun listening to a lot of jazz in college, so it was only a matter of time before it began to influence my music. The piece was conceived as a straight-ahead jazz waltz, with ample opportunity for instrumental improvisation or even scat singing if one is so inspired. Arnie Lawrence, one of the greatest saxophone players of his time, played Coltrane-inspired sheets of sound at the premiere. I was in heaven, though several of my professors were unimpressed. The piece was recently published in the Transcontinental Music songbook *High Holy Days Anthology Volume I* (2020), with its rough edges smoothed, much more appropriate for Yom Kippur. (JK)

The Kippah Song The 1970s was a time when many young Jews—myself included—were seeking a deeper connection with Jewish tradition. When Susan Nanus and I wrote this song about wearing a kippah, and when Danny and I began singing it, we had no idea that it would have the effect it had. We heard from many who told us that the simple action of donning a kippah magnified their Jewish pride. One day I received an article in the mail clipped from a university newspaper. A college student, writing about his own Jewish journey, quoted some lines from our song, and wrote, "I had begun to be more actively involved in Jewish-oriented activities...but I never began to understand the significance of this action until I heard it stated so simply and succinctly in the song." (JK)

K'shoshanah This is the third song of my Israeli *Shir HaShirim* (Song of Songs) trilogy (along with "Hanitzanim" and "Anah Halach Dodeich"). I have wonderful memories of singing it with Israeli students from the Leo Baeck High School in Haifa to welcome Shabbat. (JK)

Laasok B'divrei Torah For the CAJE conference of 1985, held near Chicago, I was invited to compose a new melody to inaugurate the conference. Since returning from Israel a few years earlier, my songwriting had been influenced by the Israeli-flamenco style of David Broza. As in most of my music, the ability to sing along is a main objective. Writing music for blessings is a tricky endeavor: How do you make "Baruch atah Adonai..." sound fresh and new each time? Luckily, the three concluding words of this blessing lent themselves to a very singable chorus, which led to this song becoming "traditional" in many day schools and camps. (JK)

Lailah Tov The bedtime story or song is a sacred ritual in the life of a child. Singing with my young children every night was so much more meaningful than performing concerts for thousands. This song was improvised one evening as I serenaded my then-five-year-old daughter Rachel. (JK)

Lamdeini Elohai (Teach Me to Pray) Lea Goldberg was one of modern Israel's greatest writers, and her poem "Lamdeini Elohai" has appeared in several different prayer books. Like a number of contemporary poets, such as Mary Oliver and Leonard Cohen, her work occupies a space somewhere between secular and sacred. In all my settings of modern Israeli poetry I have tried to bring out something of an Israeli character in the music, which is impossible to quantify; it is something that lights up the soul when you hear it. (JK)

L'chah Dodi "Do we really need another 'L'chah Dodi'?" asked a friend of mine, as she proceeded to introduce her own melody for the iconic *Kabbalat Shabbat piyut*. These metrical songs—*piyutim*—such as "Adon Olam," "L'chah Dodi," and thousands of others, make the siddur pulse with energy and spirit. No, we don't need another "L'chah Dodi," but each new melody adds excitement and joy to our Shabbat celebration. (JK)

L'chu N'ran'nah Shlomo Carlebach's influence looms large in the story of our music. In the late 1950s and throughout the '60s, he invented a new kind of Jewish song, combining Chasidic, European, Israeli, and American folk elements to create catchy, repetitive melodies that appealed to masses of young Jews searching for spiritual expression. His influence led to the creation of Israel's Chassidic Song Festival, many of whose popular tunes were subsequently adapted for Reform worship in the 1970s. A decade later, Craig Taubman in Los Angeles followed Carlebach's example by creating exciting worship services with an American sound that ignited interest in synagogue worship bands. Inspired by Taubman's efforts, I fashioned "L'chu N'ran'nah" as an opening song for *Kabbalat Shabbat* that was both joyous and instantly singable. (JK)

Leidah Hi Reishit (Birth Is a Beginning) This beautiful poem by Rabbi Alvin Fine is an essential part of contemporary Reform liturgy. I have recited it at countless funerals and memorials. But instead of being a Hebrew poem translated into English, Fine's original English was sensitively translated into Hebrew by Rabbi Simeon Maslin, *z"l*, and published in the CCAR Press's *Rabbi's Manual*. When a text calls out to me with a rhythmic flow and rhyme scheme, it is impossible to ignore. (JK)

Lirdof Tzedek (Blessing for Social Justice) Rabbi David Saperstein has done more to advance the cause of Jewish social justice than almost anyone, except perhaps his mentor, Albert Vorspan, *z"l*, (longtime director of the Reform Movement's Religious Action Center in Washington, DC, which David led for forty years). He suggested I compose a melody for this contemporary Hebrew blessing, which reminds us that justice is not a given, it is a continual pursuit. (JK)

Lo Alecha This classic text from *Pirkei Avot* says it all: It's not our responsibility to fix all the problems of this world, but we ignore them at our peril. Starting the work is the responsibility of every Jew. This song has traveled across the Jewish world more than any other of our compositions. Often assumed to be a "traditional" Jewish song, some publications have attributed it as a Chasidic melody. Still others have attached the melody for "Sheyibaneh Beit Hamikdash"—an unlikely combination of this universalist aphorism with a particularistic messianic hope for the rebuilding of the Temple. From this we learned that one can never control how one's creative work will be appropriated and used by others. (DF)

Lo Bashamayim Hi This verse from Deuteronomy is one of my favorites in the Torah. Though I usually try to write simple, straightforward tunes, "Lo Bashamayim Hi" seems to have expanded along the way. This is reflected in the recording (featuring great harmonies from Cantor Riki Lippitz), which is as big a production number as we have ever done. (JK)

Maariv Aravim In art, complexity has its purpose, but simplicity is on a higher level most of the time, I believe. Songs that can be sung by people of all ages and abilities without the need for long rehearsals is what I have most often tried to create. This version of "Maariv Aravim" was intended to be easy to learn and satisfying to sing, as well as being harmonically interesting and prayerful. (JK)

Mah Tovu For two years beginning in 1973, Danny and I wrote songs together at every opportunity. So when he traveled to Israel for his first year of rabbinical school, I was on my own as a songwriter, thus "Mah Tovu" was my first solo composing attempt since high school. As usual, I used the rhythm of the text to guide my melody. The choice of 6/8 (jazz waltz) happened by accident, as did the unconventional opening chords of A to C. When Danny came back and I played him the song, he liked the refrain but thought my verse melodies were too complicated, so I ended up using a simpler melody for each of the three verses. The song was eventually published, and I learned a valuable lesson: simplify, simplify, simplify. (JK)

The Mezuzah Song What can you say about a mezuzah beyond, "Some parchment in a little case, found in every Jewish place…"? Unlike some of my so-called children's songs ("Rabbi Ben Bag Bag" for instance) that are enjoyable—or at least endurable—by adults, this one is strictly for the younger set. (JK)

Mi Amar When I arrived in Haifa in 1981 to begin a year at the Leo Baeck High School, I was introduced to Tzeira Trifon, *z"l*, a veteran educator and principal of the middle school. Tzeira became my Israeli guide, Hebrew tutor, friend, and muse. She fought in Israel's War of Independence, then became a writer, publishing articles and poems before embarking on a career in education. Tzeira and I would meet regularly to read Hebrew poetry and talk about Israeli history and culture. She wrote several poems for me and encouraged me to set them to music. This one is my favorite. (JK)

Mi Chamochah Melody, harmony, and rhythm are the three elements of music. We usually think of melody as being primary, but that is because our brains rely on a string of musical notes to identify one tune from the next. Of course, melody is crucial, but it's actually rhythm that grabs us, pushes us through the door, and takes us on our musical journey. Just as Miriam played her timbral, an ancient percussion instrument, so do we use Middle Eastern rhythms to punctuate this song of freedom from our Torah. (JK)

Modeh Ani By 1972, the music of Debbie Friedman was beginning to catch on throughout the Reform Movement's camps and synagogues. I had written a few liturgical tunes in high school, but "Modeh Ani" was Danny's and my first attempt to compose a song in the new style. Our intention was to write a catchy melody for this prayer that could be sung by kids in religious school or camp. The melody was composed in real time, trying different note combinations and chords over and over until a singable tune emerged that we were happy with. To our delight, the song was such a hit at camp in the summer of 1973 that it was chosen to appear on the second *Songs NFTY Sings* LP, and thus was our songwriting partnership launched. (JK)

Modim Anachnu Lach In my view, the siddur is much more than a guide to prayer; it is an expression of our shared values, a songbook of the soul. The idea of giving thanks is as old as humanity. When we sing these words, we open our hearts to the very real possibility that our thoughts and actions can make us better people and the world a better place. (JK)

My Sukkah There are many wonderful holiday songs. Some are based on feelings associated with the day, while others teach or explain the holiday itself. And many songs try to do both, which can be more challenging for the composer. Often, our goal is to create a song that's fun to sing that also teaches something about the holiday. This song for Sukkot focuses on the significance of the sukkah itself, emphasizing the tradition of welcoming guests, called *ushpizin*. (JK)

Open Up Our Eyes This prayer melody, a *kavanah* to precede the recitation of "Sh'ma," contains just four separate notes and a few short English phrases. The title comes from the phrase "v'ha-eir eineinu" in the morning prayer *Ahavah Rabbah*, meaning "enlighten our eyes," which was also the title of a popular song by Shlomo Carlebach. Our song was initially written for religious school services but has since evolved to become more meditative. The simple English phrases took a long time to solidify. Every word has to fit like a puzzle. (JK)

Or Zarua This song, along with "Mah Tovu," was the result of my first solo songwriting attempt after I moved back to New York to begin cantorial studies at HUC-JIR in 1974. "Or Zarua," from Psalm 97, is a verse literally bursting with potential, reflecting the light of Creation for all those with an "upright heart." We recite it during *Kabbalat Shabbat* and also at the beginning of Yom Kippur. The song's energetic melody and rhythm follow the trend of our previous dozen or so tunes: simple and catchy, easy to teach and sing. In other words, perfect for a camp song session. (JK)

Oseh Shalom Of all the songs that I composed in Haifa (1981–82) this one has the most interesting history. The tune was originally intended for the prayer "V'timloch Atah" from the Rosh HaShanah *Amidah*. As the melody emerged, I remember thinking it sounded like something Debbie Friedman would write, even wondering if I had unconsciously stolen it from her (though I hadn't). After the High Holy Days that year, one of my students mentioned how much he liked the new tune and wished we could sing it more often, but I felt uncomfortable singing those particular words apart from worship. In 1982, back in the States, Danny and I wanted to sing the new song, but with a different text. One evening, while driving to a concert, we sang the tune over and over using every Hebrew prayer we could think of for the lyrics, until we settled on "Oseh Shalom," but not before making a minor adjustment, repeating the word *shalom*, a change so subtle it is hardly noticeable. The phrase "v'al kol yoshvei teiveil" (and for all humanity) was added to the text some two decades later. We are deeply humbled that this prayer for peace has became one of our most popular and enduring songs. (JK)

Planting Song In the mid-1980s, I was cantor of a synagogue near Chicago and did some music work with a production team doing kids' television programs for the Jewish Federation. At one point I was asked to write music for an unfinished lyric about trees, written by one of the actors. I gave it a try, without success. Fast-forward a couple of years. I needed to come up with a new song for Tu BiShvat on a deadline. I looked through my files, found the old lyrics, finished the song, but neglected to properly credit the author of those words. That was a mistake, and I have since apologized to my unwitting collaborator, who just happens to be the voice of television's Homer Simpson. Thank you, Dan Castellaneta! (JK)

Pursuer of Peace What is a protest song? Bob Dylan once famously said (I'm paraphrasing), "I don't write 'protest' songs; all my songs are love songs." Beyond his sarcasm is a truth: We can protest (and sing) against injustice, but only when we rise above our hate and fear will we achieve that better world for which we pray. Rabbi Hillel's famous dictum ("If not now, when?") serves as a proof text. (JK)

Rabbi Ben Bag Bag Ben Bag Bag was a real person, and sadly, we know virtually nothing about him, the rabbi whose admonition to "turn it again"—referring to the Torah—is one of the Talmud's most quoted maxims. The song began as a cute rhyme I came up with to amuse my (then) young daughters, riffing on "Bag Bag" and his double "name-name." Turning the rhyme into a song was not hard, though I never expected it to become a fan favorite. At one CAJE conference a Chabad rabbi thanked me for writing it, and years later, someone in England actually translated the entire song into Yiddish! (JK)

Ruth and Naomi The saga of Ruth is one of the most poignant stories in our tradition. We read *The Book of Ruth* each year during Shavuot, thus our song provides a musical commentary to the reading. We also wanted to highlight the importance of welcoming those who have chosen to join the Jewish people. Coming from a different background, Ruth's devotion has been an inspiration to millions who have echoed her famous words, "Your people shall be my people." (JK)

Shabbat HaMalkah Some years ago, I was asked to compose a song in honor of Rabbi Rosalind Gold on the occasion of her retirement. For my text I selected Bialik's beloved poem that heralds Shabbat, metaphorically, in the figure of the Sabbath Queen. I intentionally imitated the melodic style of the late Naomi Shemer, Israel's foremost songwriter, whose songs will forever evoke the land and the spirit of Israel. (JK)

Shalom Rav Like a number of our initial songs, "Shalom Rav" was inspired by the desire to create meaningful worship music for a new generation of Jewish teens in the early 1970s. Our songwriting sessions usually began with Danny picking up the *Union Prayer Book*, a siddur small enough to hold in one hand, having been used continually by Reform Jews (with revisions of course) since 1895. He would flip through the pages, looking for prayers to set to music. The text selected, Danny would translate the Hebrew for my benefit, and I would begin playing chords until we heard an interesting progression. We listened to and followed each other, as Danny's voice searched for a melody within the chords, going back and forth, tweaking and refining the tune until we were satisfied. Sometimes I would have a cassette recorder handy to record our work, but if I forgot, we would have to sing the new tune repeatedly until it was memorized. Luckily, on that day in the fall of 1973, I did have a tape recorder running when Danny and I met at my apartment to finish "Shalom Rav." On the tape (which you can hear on our website) there is excitement in our voices as the second verse takes shape and the entire song is completed. From that moment on, we sang (and have sung) the song everywhere, in synagogues and churches, schools and camps, in preschools and nursing homes, for baby namings, weddings, and funerals, with banjos and bongos, orchestras and choirs, and sometimes with no instruments at all. We have been blessed to hear hundreds of thoughtful interpretations from a legion of talented (and mostly younger) musicians. Hearing you sing our song is a treasured gift to us! Yet, in spite of the awesome power of song, the peace of "Shalom Rav" is still, sadly, beyond our reach. It will only come when we truly make peace with ourselves, with our neighbors, and with the world. (JK)

* * *

Writing in late 2023, fifty years after writing "**Shalom Rav**," I can't help but remember the trauma and confusion we felt during and following the Yom Kippur War. I was a cantorial soloist at a congregation in Wellesley, Massachusetts, and the Hillel advisor at Wellesley College. The Jewish songs we knew at the time were celebratory and didn't feel appropriate or hopeful as we absorbed what had happened in Israel. "Shalom Rav" evokes the reflective, prayerful desire we felt to use music to process our feelings. It quickly became *the* anthem of so many camps and youth movements. I remember the instinctive reaction to folks singing the tune to put their hands around their neighbors' shoulder and sway as they sang. As these young people moved into Jewish congregations, they brought this melody with them, and it has become a synagogue standard in North America and around the Jewish world. Its message resonated as strongly after October 7, 2023, as it did in the fall of 1973. (DF)

Shavua Tov, May You Have a Good Week Here is another tune that began as a religious school teaching song but over the years has carved out a place for itself in many camps, youth groups, and synagogues. It captures that sublime experience of watching, smelling, and tasting the essence of Shabbat slipping away in real time. In spite of its simple melody and lyrics, this song works as ritual, proving that composers may create the songs, but people will ultimately choose whether (or not) to sing them and, more importantly, how. (JK)

Shehecheyanu I There can be no more appropriate blessing for our fiftieth anniversary and the publication of this anthology than "Shehecheyanu." To say that Danny and I are grateful to arrive at this moment in time is an understatement! This particular setting began as a commission for a wedding. I have since sung it at many sacred occasions, and I hope you and your singers will be able to experience this joyful sound in your community. (JK)

Shehecheyanu II (Thank You, God) I had one simple goal in writing this song for young children: to teach them how to pronounce three of the hardest multi-syllable words in our liturgy and to learn what they mean. To accomplish this, I turned to one of the oldest musical tricks in the book: the call and response. Then, to spice up the song and make it fun to sing, I incorporated the so-called Bo Diddley rhythm, which Bruce Springsteen has whimsically called "the heartbeat of the universe." (JK)

Sh'ma Koleinu Among the songs I composed for my HUC-JIR senior recital, this one is unique: the only one written in a major key. Changing the tonality gave me an opportunity to bring a different sound into the *S'lichot* service. The key of D major aligns with the mid-twentieth-century American folk tradition in which I grew up. In the end, neither major nor minor has the last word. They are two sides of a single coin, and we could not exist without them both. (JK)

Shomeir Yisrael As I am fond of saying, "The song goes where it wants to go." Yes, I know that songs are not living creatures, but sometimes I wonder... When a song really starts to emerge, which can be instantaneous or after a long process, it reveals a style and takes on an identity. As this melody emerged out of the ashes of a previous version that failed to excite me, I wondered where it came from, as I had never written anything remotely like it, and probably never will again. (JK)

Sim Shalom Several of the songs published here are rewrites, songs that sound nothing like they did when first written. (These include "L'chah Dodi," "Shomeir Yisrael," "Yom Chadash," and this one). It's not that the originals weren't good, just that they lacked a certain something. Looking back, in many cases the originals were too slow, lacking sufficient motion. If I was (insert name of a famous songwriter), then everyone would want to hear those older versions. But I'm not, so please, just sing and enjoy! (JK)

Sin'u Ra Like a number of other songs of ours, this one is a mashup of two different biblical verses that (in this case) we found nested together in the *Union Prayer Book*. And what powerful verses they are: "Proclaim liberty throughout the land," words from Leviticus inscribed on the Liberty Bell, paired with Amos's prophetic admonition, "Hate evil and love the good." If only everyone followed these words, if only... (JK)

The Synagogue The Jewish world is complex, with lots of moving parts. You may remember the emotional debates some years ago concerning which of our institutions were most crucial for Jewish survival. I agree with those who said that synagogues make Jews, while the other institutions use them. One thing we can all agree on is that synagogues are essential, and this educational song for children explains why. (JK)

Ten Commandments I'm not very good at math, but there is something about ten that calls to me—perhaps because the number ten aligns with our body's fingers and toes, not to mention the ten *s'firot* in Kabbalah. Is it important to know the Ten Commandments by heart? I think it is, which is why Rabbi Jeff Salkin and I wrote this song, with a rhyme for each one, appropriate for children, of course. (JK)

The Ten Plagues What's the point of memorizing anything when technology ensures that everything we need to know is available in an instant? If you wanted to know the order of the Ten Plagues (without consulting the internet) you could simply sing this song, if you have it memorized, that is. (JK)

This Is Very Good In 1974, Danny and I began our studies at HUC-JIR, and in 1975, the Reform Movement inaugurated *Gates of Prayer*, the first new Reform siddur in almost eighty years. Today, *GOP* is all but forgotten, yet at the time, its many innovations delighted worship leaders: song transliterations (in the back of the book), much more Hebrew, new readings for special occasions, and most interestingly for me, modern liturgical poetry, written principally by editor Rabbi Chaim Stern. One of the Shabbat services (for families) began with this charming poem about the world's creation. I could see right away that "This is very good" would make a fun and singable chorus, while the rejoinder "Like God we love..." could serve as a contrasting bridge. The melody came quickly, and the references to different animals (...and APES!) gave the song a playfulness that endeared it to children at camp and in synagogue. (JK)

The Torah (Eitz Chayim Hi) Here is another of my mid-1970s songs written for ARE. It's a simple song with a simple teaching, and a nice way to introduce the words and meaning of *eitz chayim* / "tree of life" to children. (JK)

Tov L'hodot One of our earliest efforts, this song shares an interesting feature with several others we've written ("Yism'chu," for example) in having a repetitive chorus and verses that feature contrasting melodies. That's not very common in folk-style music. While the chorus could not be simpler (and it's clearly influenced by rock 'n' roll), the verses are a little more adventurous in setting the biblical Hebrew, experimenting with tonality and phrasing. (JK)

Tzadik Katamar Songs on the drawing board end up going where they want to go. In a similar vein, Leonard Bernstein used to talk about the inevitability of music, suggesting that there are forces beyond our awareness or understanding that eventually determine the result of our efforts. All this is to say that this setting of "Tzadik Katamar" turned out differently than I had intended. I was reaching for something simpler, more intimate, but the song had another idea, and all I could do was follow. (JK)

Ushmor "Ushmor" might not be as well-known as "Shalom Rav," but it was written during that time and shares similar qualities. Like "Shalom Rav," its opening phrase announces something new: in this case, an easy-going, vaguely Brazilian pop rhythm with jazz-inflected chords, a sweet melody reminiscent of prayer-chant, and an attitude that quietly proclaims, "This is our siddur, too!" Most important, I believe the key to understanding "Ushmor" is the quest for intimacy—with God and with one another. (JK)

V'ahavta L'rei-acha Kamocha In early 1981, soon after my ordination, I got a phone call that would change my life when Rabbi Robert Samuels invited me to come to the Leo Baeck School in Haifa, where he was headmaster. In addition to my working with students and serving as the school's cantor-in-residence, Bob urged me to compose new music for the Israeli Reform Movement, the results of which are found throughout this anthology. Rabbi Samuels became my mentor and lifelong friend. Ten years later, he called to tell me that the Leo Baeck Education Center had won a prestigious award, the Buber-Rosenzweig Prize, presented each year in Germany to individuals and organizations working toward Christian-Jewish understanding. He asked if I would write a new song for the occasion that the Leo Baeck students would sing. Here is the song I wrote, which is dedicated to his memory. (JK)

V'al Kulam It may sound incongruous that a piece written according to *nusach* (the traditional prayer mode, in this case for the High Holy Days) would be featured in my "jazz service" for *S'lichot*. Jazz is as much a concept as a form. It is an approach to music, encompassing dialogue, space, freedom, and invention. Traditional cantors have been compared to jazz musicians in the way they improvise around the *nusach*, exploring the music of the soul, expressing the prayer of the heart. There is, or should be, an element of jazz in everything we sing. All we need to do is reach for it. (JK)

V'eirastich Li No more beautiful expression of love for God can be found than this prophetic text from Hosea. It is recited as one wraps *t'fillin* and is often sung when couples unite in marriage. We wrote this melody for the wedding of two close friends. (JK)

V'sham'ru Let's talk about modes. While most of the songs we sing are in major or minor keys, composers sometimes borrow scales from other musical traditions, opening the possibility of subtle melodic changes due to the altered scale. Here's a good example: This "V'shamru" is in mixolydian mode, which simply means that (in the key of C) we would sing a B-flat instead of B-natural. You can hear this in the phrase "v'nei Yisrael." There was no plan, it was just an aesthetic choice because I liked the sound. (JK)

V'yashvu Ish If I remember correctly (it was over fifty years ago), this was the fourth or fifth song we wrote together. Finding the words in the *Union Prayer Book*, we chose the text because we loved the meaning. Afterward, we appended the companion verse, "Lo Yisa Goi." As you can hear, we were experimenting with chord progressions and modes, not to mention spicing up the song with a Cmaj7 chord, not something you would commonly hear at a camp song session. A couple of years later (1976) we entered the song in a US Bicentennial song contest sponsored by the National Jewish Welfare Board, and to our amazement, we won! (JK)

V'zot HaTorah Growing up in a classical Reform synagogue, I never got to experience the choreography that animates so many synagogue rituals. Later on, as I visited different Jewish communities, I came to appreciate the gestures and motions that abound in traditional worship spaces. One of the most interesting is the symbolic kissing of the Torah during its procession after the reading, when everyone reaches into the aisle, trying to touch the scroll with their tallit. But the most powerful moment is the raising of the Torah, *hagbaah*, when people point their curved pinky (imitating the letter *yod*, symbolizing God's name) toward the open scroll. It is challenging to portray such a powerful moment in song, but we tried. (JK)

We Are Counting (A Song for the Omer) This song was written for the counting of the forty-nine days between Pesach and Shavuot, called *S'firat HaOmer*. While it's rare for me to consciously copy the style of a popular composer, I do detect the subtle influence of Paul Simon here, which hardly surprises me, since he writes and sings about journeys in such a beautiful way. (JK)

We Are Partners Some years ago I was asked to compose a song for a couple looking forward to celebrating a milestone wedding anniversary. I thought back to my own wedding, when my friend, storyteller Syd Lieberman, *z"l*, gifted Deeana and me with a recitation of Rabbi Marc Gellman's short story called "Partners." Gellman's story is a midrash on *B'reishit* (Genesis), teaching us that we humans are God's partners in creating the world. Beginning with that idea, the song took on a life of its own, evolving into an anthem about the sacred partnership between God and humanity, reflecting our responsibilities to each other and to the fragile planet we share. I later realized it would make a nice confirmation anthem, and for that, it was perfect. (JK)

We Remember Them This song, adapted from a memorial reading in *Mishkan T'filah* by Sylvan Kamens and Rabbi Jack Reimer, underscores how our liturgy has evolved over the past half-century to incorporate modern poetry and other non-liturgical sources. If you compare the lyrics with the text in *Mishkan T'filah*, you'll see that I set only the beginning words of each line. As the words became song, they took on the character of metrical chant (see "Baruch She-amar"). The dirgelike rhythm is also significant, as is the repetition of musical phrases, inviting participation. None of this was planned in advance; it's how the song took shape as it developed. (JK)

We Say Shehecheyanu (Thank You, God) Here is an anthem for the kindergarten class, a nice way to celebrate their initial year of Jewish learning, either for consecration or graduation to first grade. (JK)

We Will Be Free It was December of 1987, and I was sitting in the Skokie kitchen of mandolin-fiddle player Stuart Rosenberg, *z"l*, discussing what we might play for an upcoming Shabbat service honoring Martin Luther King, Jr.'s birthday, recently declared a national holiday. "Let's write a song," he said, and so we did. "We Will Be Free" proudly wears its major influence, Bob Dylan's "Blowing in the Wind." In 1963 Peter, Paul and Mary sang that song at the March on Washington, and my late father, Larry, was one of many thousands in the crowd. "We Will be Free" recalls that time and gives us hope that Dr. King's dream will someday be realized. (JK)

With My Family From the 1970s collection *To See the World Through Jewish Eyes* comes this song for young children, suggested by Rabbi Daniel Syme. For this song I wanted to draw a connection for children between fun family Jewish activities and the sacred songs that accompany them. (JK)

Yeish Kochavim (There Are Stars) During my year living in Haifa, 1981–82, I encountered these celestial words by Hannah Szenesh in the Israeli Reform Movement siddur, where it preceded the "Mourner's Kaddish." The melody took shape slowly, but the song was not truly completed until Danny and I created a singable English verse a few years later. Along with several other songs from my Israel year (see "Lamdeini Elohai"), this tune brought out a more melodic and harmonically interesting style that was very much influenced by Israeli songwriters such as Yehudit Ravitz and Mati Caspi. (JK)

Yism'chu I have probably experienced more joy from the Beatles than any other music. Their influence can be found in many of our songs, with "Yism'chu" being one of the most obvious. As with most of our songs, singability is essential. While the chorus begins with a bright G major chord, the first verse switches to minor, while the second verse is in mixolydian mode similar to the chorus of "Shalom Rav." Structurally, the song follows the pattern of "Shalom Rav," where the opening line serves as a chorus, while the remaining text is divided into two verses with different melodies, composed to reflect both the phrasing and meaning of the words. (JK)

Yom Chadash (Shir Yahel) In 1977, the worldwide Reform Movement established Kibbutz Yahel in the Arava desert, and its founding members included friends from NFTY and Kutz Camp. Living in the desert is not for everyone, but over the course of my visits to Yahel, and her younger companion, Kibbutz Lotan, I experienced the deep spiritual connection to the land, the people Israel, and my Reform brothers and sisters. An Israeli educator, Gidon Elad, *z"l*, expressed the beauty and the meaning of Kibbutz Yahel in these simple verses that I set to music in 1982, during my year living in Israel. (JK)

Yotzeir Or Tradition dictates the recitation of one hundred blessings every day. So many blessings! Each one is a sacred spark; and when combined, they establish the framework of each day, the structure of our lives. This tune has a humble origin, simply written for my religious school's worship service. The melody contains elements of both Israeli and American musical styles. On the recording, check out Fareed Haque's amazing guitar solo. (JK)

You Are Stormwind I first met Rabbi Chaim Stern in 1975 at a program introducing the just-published *Gates of Prayer* siddur (superseded by *Mishkan T'filah* in 2007) at HUC-JIR. Among many innovations, *GOP* included a number of liturgical poems, some of them written by Rabbi Stern, who played us recordings of them set to music by jazz saxophonist Arnie Lawrence. The combination of Chaim's words and Arnie's soulful interpretations inspired me to take my own music in new directions. After my ordination, as cantor at Chaim's synagogue in Chappaqua, New York, I had the privilege of setting several of his poems written for the synagogue's thirtieth anniversary. I arranged "Stormwind" to feature Arnie Lawrence's sublime saxophone improvisations at the premiere. Several years later, Howard Levy added his own jazz improvisations to our recording. (JK)

You Can Change the World This song is about so much more than just the holiday of Purim. It is certainly a feminist anthem, but its lesson is more about the power of one individual to step up and make the world a better place. I am grateful to co-writer Rabbi Donald Rossoff for helping me bring this song into the world. (JK)

Y'varech'cha (Priestly Blessing) Songs help us to experience and remember sacred moments in our lives. My children—and Danny's too—will always recall their parents blessing them with this tune every Friday evening at the Shabbat dinner table. It is one of the oldest blessings in our tradition, holding a sacred power that we continue to pass along from each generation to the next. (JK)

Zeh Hayom Welcome to the final song in this—literally—A to Z compendium. This song is a special one. It was composed for the dedication of the Rashi School's new building in Dedham, Massachusetts, in 2010. (Rashi is the Boston area's Reform-affiliated day school, founded in 1986). These words, from Psalm 118, are familiar from the *Hallel* service for *Shalosh R'galim* (Three Festivals) and other sacred occasions. A better all-purpose text for happy occasions would be hard to find. Teach this to your junior choir and have a blast! (JK)

Kol B'Seder Discography

Shalom Rav: Kol B'Seder In Concert

(LP 1982) *Out of print. Also released on cassette and reissued on the compilation* Snapshots Volume 2

Side One:

		Kol B'Seder Anthology page:
1	Or Zarua	128
2	Entebbe (J. Glazer)	
3	Dreidle (S. Goldfarb, arr. Tayku)	
4	Mi Y'maleil (D. Friedman)	
5	Hey-Man! (S. Richards)	
6	The Kippah Song / The Bimah Song	92/31
7	Shavua Tov, May You Have a Good Week	142

Side Two:

1	Lo Alecha	110
2	Modeh Ani	123
3	Ashrei	23
4	Sin'u Ra	154
5	Ushmor	170
6	Tov L'hodot	166
7	Shalom Rav	140

Produced by Steven Simenowitz and Kol B'Seder
Recorded at URJ (UAHC) Kutz Camp, Warwick, NY
Engineered and mixed by Jim Manganaro
Cover photo: Lou Stevens
Cover design: Tom Ide

MUSICIANS:
Vocals: Dan Freelander and Jeff Klepper
Guitar: Jeff Klepper
Bass: Michael Antelis
Percussion: Robert Bond
Electric guitar: Peter Bliss
Fiddle: Jason Bergman (side one: 2)

The Bridge

(LP 1985) *Out of print. Also released on cassette and reissued on the compilation* Snapshots Volume 2

Side One:

1	V'yashvu Ish	179
2	Jerusalem Is Mine (K. Karen)	
3	Ani V'atah (A. Einstein/M. Gavrielov)	
4	Leaving Mother Russia (R. Solomon)	
5	Wonderful Time Down Here (Parody by Cliff Cohen)	
6	Hold Fast to Dreams (The Bridge)	69

Side Two:

1	Yism'chu	198
2	Hanitzanim	59
3	Holy Land Special	
4	You Are Stormwind	203
5	Oseh Shalom	129
6	Adonai Oz (Y'vareich et Amo)	9

Produced by Kol B'Seder with Howard Levy
Recorded and mixed by Tom Matthews
at Chicago Trax Studios
Art direction by Iris Barchechat

MUSICIANS:
Vocals: Dan Freelander and Jeff Klepper
Guitar: Jeff Klepper
Keyboards, saxophone, flute, mandolin, harmonica, and dumbek: Howard Levy
Electric guitar: Pat Flemming
Bass: Eric Hochberg
Drums: Mark Walker

Sparks of Torah

(Cassette 1989) *Out of print.*
Reissued on the compilation Snapshots Volume 3

Side One:

1	Ashreinu	26
2	Laasok B'divrei Torah	96
3	Mah Tovu	115
4	This Is Very Good	162
5	V'zot HaTorah	181
6	Yotzeir Or	202
7	Ruth and Naomi	136

Side Two:

1	Haporeis Sukkat Shalom	61
2	Kosher (Parody by Jeff Klepper and Pamela Gellen)	
3	Hashiveinu	62
4	Al Sh'loshah D'varim I (HaOlam Omeid)	15
5	We Say Shehecheyanu (Thank You, God)	187
6	Y'varech'cha (Priestly Blessing)	207
7	Eilu D'varim	46

Produced by Jeff Klepper
with Dan Freelander and Howard Levy
Engineered and mixed by Benj Kanters
at Studio Media, Evanston, IL
Vocal arrangements by Kol B'seder
Art direction by Neiger Design, Inc.
Cover photo by Steve Goodman

MUSICIANS:
Vocals: Dan Freelander and Jeff Klepper
Guitar: Jeff Klepper
Keyboards and harmonica: Howard Levy
Bass: Larry Gray
Drums: Mark Walker
Drums: Phil Gratteau
Lead guitar: Fareed Haque
Percussion: Alejo Poveda

Growin' Volume I

(Cassette 1991) *Out of print.*
Reissued on the compilation Songs for Growin'

Side One:

1	Heveinu (D. Feingold)	
2	With My Family	192
3	I'm Growin'	77
4	Af, Peh, Ozen (Parts of My Body)	10
5	The Mezuzah Song	118
6	The Kippah Song	92
7	Adon Olam (U. Hitman)	
8	We Say Shehecheyanu (Thank You, God)	187

Side Two:

1	Modeh Ani	123
2	Yotzeir Or	202
3	Boker Tov, Shalom Shalom	
4	Maariv Aravim	114
5	The Bimah Song	31
6	Laasok B'divrei Torah	96
7	Again and Again (*Amidah* for Children)	12

Produced by Kol B'Seder
Recorded 1991 at Studio Media, Evanston, IL,
by Benj Kantors
Cover photo: Steve Goodman
Cover art: Neiger Design Inc.

MUSICIANS:
Vocals: Dan Freelander and Jeff Klepper
Guitar: Jeff Klepper
Bass: Larry Gray
Drums: Mark Walker
Keyboards: Fred Simon
Lead guitar: Dave Onderdonk
Lead guitar: Fareed Haque (side two: 2, 6)
Flute: Steve Eisen
Harmonica: Howard Levy

Growin' Volume II

(Cassette 1991) *Out of print.*
Reissued on the compilation Songs for Growin'

Side One:

1	In the Beginning	82
2	Jonah	88
3	My Sukkah	125
4	The Torah (Eitz Chayim Hi)	164
5	Chanukah Lights	35
6	Planting Song	130
7	Hey-Man! (S. Richards)	
8	Shehecheyanu (Tz. Pik)	

Side Two:

1	You Can Change the World	205
2	The Ten Plagues	160
3	Ten Commandments	158
4	Mah Yafeh Hayom (I. Miron)	
5	Shir Hamaalot-Shabbat Shalom (C. Taubman)	
6	L'chah Dodi	101
7	Shavua Tov, May You Have a Good Week	142

Produced by Kol B'Seder
Recorded 1991 at Studio Media, Evanston, IL,
by Benj Kantors
Cover photo: Steve Goodman
Cover art: Neiger Design Inc.

MUSICIANS:
Vocals: Dan Freelander and Jeff Klepper
Guitar: Jeff Klepper
Bass: Larry Gray
Drums: Mark Walker
Keyboards: Fred Simon
Lead guitar: Dave Onderdonk
Flute: Steve Eisen
Harmonica and mandolin: Howard Levy

In Every Generation

(CD 1993) *Out of print. Also released on cassette and reissued on the compilation* Snapshots Volume 3

1	Im Ein Ani Li	75
2	In Every Generation (B'chol Dor Vador)	79
3	Lo Bashamayim Hi	111
4	Halomeid	56
5	V'eirastich Li	175
6	Another Year, Another Chanukah	20
7	Ashrei Adam Matza Chochmah	24
8	Coming Home	39
9	Lo Alecha	110
10	Al Sh'loshah D'varim II (HaOlam Kayam)	17
11	We Didn't Start No Trouble (Parody by Jeff Klepper, Jeff Salkin, and Jeffrey Mallow)	
12	Yeish Kochavim (There Are Stars)	195

Recorded at Studio Media, Evanston, IL
by Benj Kanters and Scott Steinman
Produced by Jeff Klepper and Benj Kanters
Vocal arrangements by Kol B'Seder
Mixed by John Buehler
Mastered at Classic Digital, Evanston, IL
Cover photo by Cindy Levitt

MUSICIANS:
Vocals: Dan Freelander and Jeff Klepper
Vocals: Riki Lippitz (1, 3, 6, 8)
Guitar and Tambourine: Jeff Klepper
Bass: Eric Hochberg
Bass: Larry Gray (7, 9, 12)
Piano: Peter Saks
Piano: Fred Simon (7, 9, 12)
Drums: Jeff Thomas
Drums: Mark Walker (7, 9, 12)
Harmonica: Howard Levy
Percussion: Noah Sheldon
Lead guitar: Fareed Haque
Electric guitar: Dave Onderdonk (7, 9, 12)
Soprano sax and flute: Steve Zoloto
Tenor sax: Steve Eisen (9)
Fiddle and mandolin: Stuart Rosenberg (8)

We Are Partners
(CD and Digital 2024)

"Side" One: Liturgy

1	Shehecheyanu I	144
2	Chatzi Kaddish *	36
3	Avinu Malkeinu	27
4	Sim Shalom	151
5	B'sefer Chayim	33
6	Ki Anu Amecha	90
7	Baruch She-amar	28
8	L'chu N'ran'nah	104
9	Shomeir Yisrael	149
10	Ilu Finu	73
11	V'al Kulam	174
12	Hodo al Eretz	68
13	Aleinu *	18
14	Healing Prayer (Adonai Y'vareich) *	64
15	Zeh Hayom	209
16	Adonai, Adonai	8

"Side" Two: Times and Seasons

17	V'ahavta L'rei-acha Kamocha	172
18	Lirdof Tzedek (Blessing for Social Justice) *	108
19	Pursuer of Peace	132
20	Chazak, Chazak	38
21	Jeff's Nigun	87
22	Shabbat HaMalkah *	138
23	Eichah Ashir	44
24	We Are Counting (A Song for the Omer) *	182
25	I Will Plant for My Children (Honi's Song) *	71
26	Cowboy Jew from Mars *	42
27	Shehecheyanu II (Thank You, God)	146
28	We Remember Them	185
29	We Are Partners *	184
30	Lailah Tov *	98

Recorded and mixed at
Wellspring Sound, Acton, MA (2024)
Produced by Joe Eglash and Jeff Klepper
Engineered by Eric Kilburn with Josh Lu
Cover art by David Billotti
Special thanks to guest vocalist Cantor Shanna Zell

* Recorded at Long Dog Studios, Skokie, IL (2004)
Produced by Stuart Rosenberg
Engineered by Mike Konopka
Overdubs recorded and mixed at Wellspring Sound
by Eric Kilburn (2024)

MUSICIANS:
Vocals: Dan Freelander and Jeff Klepper
Vocals: Shanna Zell (3, 17, 18, 27, 28, 29)
Vocals on *Shehecheyanu I*: Dan Freelander; Cantors Lisa Doob, DJ Fortine, Becky Khitrik, and Shanna Zell
Guitar: Jeff Klepper
Electric Guitar: Eric Kilburn (15, 18, 27)
Lead Guitar: Joe Eglash (17, 29)
Lead Guitar: Eric Kilburn (1, 3, 4, 15, 23)
Drums: Morris Jennings (2004)
Drums: John Dorizzi (2024)
Bass: Dick Bunn (2004)
Bass: Peter Allard (2024)
Percussion: Paul Wertico (2004)
Percussion: John Dorizzi, Jeff Klepper (2024)
Keyboard: Barbara Wertico (18, 24)
Keyboard: Brad Hatfield (9, 11, 17, 20, 26, 28)
Keyboard: Chris Mahieu (16)
Mandolin: Stuart Rosenberg (30)
Mandolin: Eric Kilburn (25)

Recording the We Are Partners *album at Wellspring Sound, Acton, Massachusetts, January 2024. Left to right: Eric Kilburn (engineer), Joe Eglash (producer), Dan, and Jeff (seated)*

Jeff Klepper Solo Discography

Yom Chadash

(Cassette 1988) *Out of print.*
Reissued on Yom Chadash *CD*

Side One:

1	Mi Amar	119
2	Haneirot Halalu	58
3	K'shoshanah	94
4	Anah Halach Dodeich	19
5	Hanitzanim	59
6	Lamdeini Elohai (Teach Me to Pray)	99
7	Tzadik Katamar	168

Side Two:

1	Yom Chadash (Shir Yahel)	200
2	Haporeis Sukkat Shalom	61
3	Oseh Shalom	129
4	Bayom Hahu	30
5	Yeish Kochavim (There Are Stars)	195
6	Adon Olam	5

Recorded 1988 by Benj Kantors
at Studio Media, Evanston, IL
Produced by Jeff Klepper

MUSICIANS:
Guitar and vocals: Jeff Klepper
Piano, harmonica, flute, saxophone, and mandolin: Howard Levy
Bass: Eric Hochberg
Drums: Jeff Thomas

In This Place: Jewish Songs of Time and Space

(CD and Cassette 1997)

1	In This Place	84
2	You Are Stormwind	203
3	Give Me Sleep (Hashkiveinu)	54
4	Modim Anachnu Lach	124
5	Adon Olam (Traditional)	
6	Empty Chair	50
7	Nigun (Traditional)	
8	Open Up Our Eyes	127
9	Esa Einai	53
10	Elohim Y'choneinu (Psalm 67)	49
11	Ahavah Rabbah	14
12	Sh'ma Koleinu	147
13	Leidah Hi Reishit (Birth Is a Beginning)	105

Produced by Stuart Rosenberg
Engineered by Mike Konopka
Recorded 1996 at the Bat Cave, Skokie, IL
Mixed at Chicago Recording Company by Stuart Rosenberg and Mike Konopka
Cover photo by Andy Mueller
Graphics by Neiger Design Inc.

MUSICIANS:
Guitar and vocals: Jeff Klepper
Keyboard, harmonica, and dumbek: Howard Levy
String Bass: Eric Hochberg
String Bass: Kelly Sill
String Bass: Larry Gray
Hammer dulcimer: Collins Trier
Flute and saxophone: Steve Zoloto
Percussion: Alejo Poveda
Conga: Reuben Alvarez

Jeff Klepper Live In Concert: Jewish Music for the Masses
(CD 2002)

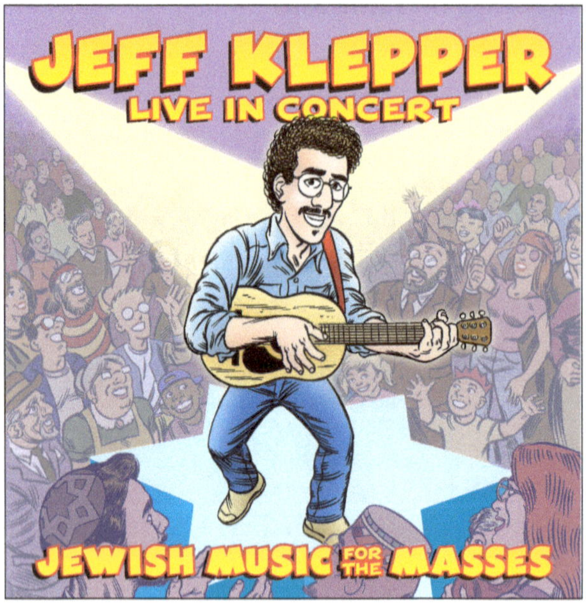

1	Hineih Mah Tov Blues	66
2	Chad Gadya (Traditional)	
3	Shabbes (Traditional), feat. Evan Harlan	
4	Adon Olam (Traditional), feat. Ilene Stahl	
5	Stuck Inside of Monsey With the Brooklyn Blues Again (Parody by Jeff Klepper)	
6	Talkin' Hava Nagila Blues (B. Dylan)	
7	Cantillation Row (Parody by Jeff Klepper)	
8	High Holy Day Blues (Parody by Jeff Klepper)	
9	Just Like a Chazzn (Parody by Jeff Klepper)	
10	Shalom Aleichem (D. Shneyer)	
11	Eit Dodim (Traditional), feat. Debbie Friedman	
12	L'chah Dodi	101
13	Coming Home	39
14	Rollin' Up the Torah (Parody by Jeff Klepper and Jeffrey Mallow)	
15	We Will Be Free, feat. Stuart Rosenberg	189
16	Empty Chair, feat. Stuart Rosenberg	50
17	In Every Generation (B'chol Dor Vador), feat. Dan Freelander	79
18	Lo Alecha, feat. Howard Levy	110
19	Bashanah Habaah (N. Hirsch/E. Manor)	
20	Rabbi Ben Bag Bag, feat. Josh Nelson	134

Produced by Jeff Klepper
with Josh Nelson and Dave Lefkowitz
Mixed and mastered by Dave Lefkowitz
Cover art: Don Simpson

Recorded live at:
1–5 Temple Reyim, Newton, MA (2002)
6, 17 North American Jewish Music Festival, Concord Hotel, Kiamisha Lake, NY (1999)
7, 14 Temple Micah, Washington, DC (1999)
8–10 URJ Kallot at Beloit College, Beloit, WI (1999, 1997)
11–13 Hava Nashira, URJ Olin-Sang-Ruby Union Institute, Oconomowoc, WI (1992)
15–16 Beth Emet The Free Synagogue, Evanston, IL (1997)
18 URJ Olin-Sang-Ruby Union Institute, Oconomowoc, WI (1991)
19 Temple Reyim, Newton, MA (2002)
20 Studio bonus track, Boston, MA (2002)

MUSICIANS:
Guitar and vocals: Jeff Klepper
Guitar and vocals: Debbie Friedman (11)
Vocals: Dan Freelander (17)
Harmonica: Jeff Klepper (7–9)
Harmonica: Howard Levy (10, 18)
Clarinet: Ilene Stahl (1–5, 19)
Accordion: Evan Harlan (1–5, 19)
Bass: Josh Nelson (1–5, 19, 20)
Bass: Michael Heimlich (18)
Percussion: Shulamit Wise Fairman (1–5, 19)
Piano: Howard Levy (9, 18)
Lead guitar: Josh Nelson (20)
Mandolin and fiddle: Stuart Rosenberg (9–10, 15–16)
Drums: Dede Sampaio (18)

Additional Recordings by Kol B'Seder

Especially Jewish Symbols
(Cassette 1977) *Out of print.*

1	The Synagogue	156
2	The Torah (Eitz Chayim Hi)	164
3	The Bimah Song	31
4	The Kippah Song	92
5	The Mezuzah Song	118
6	Shavua Tov, May You Have a Good Week	142

Published by ARE (Alternatives in Religious Education), Denver, CO
Note: Alternatives in Religious Education (ARE) created innovative curricula and materials for Jewish schools beginning in the early 1970s. Many of Kol B'Seder's educational songs were commissioned and published by ARE
Listen at kolbseder.com/archives

Bible People Songs

(Cassette 1981) *Out of print.*

This Is Very Good	162
Abraham	3
The Ten Plagues	160
Ten Commandments	158

Published by ARE (Alternatives in Religious Education), Denver, CO

To See the World Through Jewish Eyes Volume I

(LP 1979) *Out of print.*

With My Family	192
Af, Peh, Ozen (Parts of My Body)	10
We Say Shehecheyanu (Thank You, God)	187

Published by UAHC Dept. of Education, New York, NY
Note: The UAHC Department of Education revamped its religious school curriculum in the late 1970s, releasing two LPs of new music composed and recorded by Steven Carr Reuben and Jeff Klepper. A number of these songs were published in Manginot, *later reissued as* The Complete Jewish Songbook for Children Volume I *(TMP).*

To See the World Through Jewish Eyes Volume II

(LP 1984) *Out of print.*

You Can Change the World	205
I'm Growin'	77

Published by UAHC Dept. of Education, New York, NY
Listen at kolbseder.com/archives

Songs NFTY Sings series (Complete NFTY Recordings)

(Seven original albums, reissued 2003 by Transcontinental Music Publications/NFTY)

Kol B'Seder songs from
Songs NFTY Sings II: Shiru Shir Chadash (1973)

Modeh Ani	123
Ashrei	23

Kol B'Seder songs from
Songs NFTY Sings III: Ten Shabbat V'Ten Shalom (1974)

Tov L'hodot	166
V'yashvu Ish	179
Shalom Rav	140
Lo Alecha	110

Kol B'Seder songs from
NFTY IV: The Time of Singing (1977)

Or Zarua	128
Ushmor	170

Kol B'Seder songs from
Songs NFTY Sings V: This Is Very Good (1980)

Sin'u Ra	154
Adonai Oz (Y'vareich et Amo)	9
This Is Very Good	162

Kol B'Seder songs from
Songs NFTY Sings VI: Hold Fast to Dreams (1985)

Oseh Shalom	129
Mah Tovu	115
Hold Fast to Dreams	69

Kol B'Seder songs from
Songs NFTY Sings VII: Fifty Years In the Making (1989)

Eilu D'varim	46
Shavua Tov, May You Have a Good Week	142
Shalom Rav	140

American Nusach Concert

(Cassette 1986) *Out of print.*

Lo Alecha	110
V'yashvu Ish	179
Oseh Shalom	129
Laasok B'divrei Torah	96
Shalom Rav	140

From CAJE 11, University of Maryland, August 1986
Released by CAJE (Conference for the Advancement of Jewish Education)
Produced by Les Bronstein
Listen at kolbseder.com/archives

Live at CAJE 17

(Cassette 1992) *Out of print.*

Track	Page
Coming Home	39
Shalom Rav	140

Recorded at University of Southern California, August 16, 1992
Produced by Doug Cotler and Ben Zion Kogen
Mastered by Kevan Patton
Listen at kolbseder.com/archives

Sing Out for Justice

(CD 1998) *Out of print.*

Track	Page
We Will Be Free	189
Lo Alecha	110

Recorded live at UAHC Biennial, Dallas, TX, November 1, 1997
Produced by UAHC Religious Action Center, Washington, DC
Listen at kolbseder.com/archives

Yom Chadash

(CD reissue 1999)

For primary tracklist, see original release. Additional tracks:

#	Track	Page
14	Lo Yarei-u (first recording)	
15	Mi Chamochah (first recording)	121
16	Haporeis Sukkat Shalom (new recording)	61
17	V'sham'ru (first recording)	177
18	Bayom Hahu (new recording)	30
19	Oseh Shalom (new recording)	129

Recorded 1996 by Stuart Rosenberg and Mike Konopka at the Bat Cave, Skokie, IL
Cover photograph by Jeff Klepper

MUSICIANS:
Guitar and vocals: Jeff Klepper
Keyboard and dumbek: Howard Levy
Flute: Steve Zoloto (15, 16)

Songs for Growin'

(CD reissue 2002, Transcontinental Music Publications)

For tracklist, see original releases.
Published by Transcontinental Music Publications (URJ)
Cover art: Liora Klepper

Snapshots: The Best of Kol B'Seder Volume I

(CD compilation 2004)

#	Track	Page
1	Modeh Ani (*Songs for Growin'*)	123
2	Radio Interview 1	
3	Lo Alecha (*In Every Generation*)	110
4	Ushmor (new recording, 1991)	170
5	Tov L'hodot (new recording, 1991)	166
6	Radio Interview 2	
7	Or Zarua (new recording, 1991)	128
8	Ashrei (*Songs NFTY Sings II*)	23
9	Sin'u Ra (new recording, 1991)	154
10	V'yashvu Ish (work tape, 1973)	179
11	V'yashvu Ish (*The Bridge*)	179
12	Haporeis Sukkat Shalom (*Sparks of Torah*)	61
13	Oseh Shalom (*The Bridge*)	129
14	Mah Tovu (*Sparks of Torah*)	115
15	Radio Interview 3	
16	Yism'chu (*The Bridge*)	198
17	Laasok B'divrei Torah (*Sparks of Torah*)	96
18	In Every Generation (B'chol Dor Vador) (*In Every Generation*)	79
19	Radio Interview 4	
20	Eilu D'varim (*Songs NFTY Sings VII*)	46
21	Hold Fast to Dreams (The Bridge) (*Songs NFTY Sings VI*)	69
22	Yeish Kochavim (There Are Stars) (*In Every Generation*)	195
23	Radio Interview 5	
24	Shalom Rav (1978 interview)	
25	Shalom Rav (new recording, 1991)	140
26	Adonai Oz (Y'vareich et Amo) (*The Bridge*)	9
27	Shalom Rav (work tape snippets, 1973)	140

Reissue produced by Jeff Klepper
Executive producer: Jim Ball
Engineered and mastered by Dave Lefkowitz
Art direction by Alex Nosevich
Radio interview snippets from:
Jewish Viewpoint (American Jewish Committee) 1978
interviewer: Rabbi James Rudin
New recordings (1991) produced by Jeff Klepper
Recorded at Studio Media, Evanston, IL, by Benj Kantors

See original releases for additional credits
Musicians on 1, 3, 4, 5, 7, 9, 22, 25:
Guitar: Jeff Klepper
Vocals: Dan Freelander and Jeff Klepper
Bass: Larry Gray
Keyboards: Fred Simon
Drums: Mark Walker
Nylon and electric guitar: Dave Onderdonk
Tenor sax: Steve Eisen

Snapshots: The Best of Kol B'Seder Volume II (1972–1988)

(CD compilation 2011)

For primary tracklist, see original releases of Shalom Rav: Kol B'Seder Live In Concert *and* The Bridge. *Additional tracks:*

1	Sound Bites (mashup)	
25	Oseh Shalom (live 1988)	129
26	Adon Olam (U. Hitman) (live 1988)	
27	Hodu (Traditional) (1972)	
28	Y'varech'cha (Priestly Blessing) (demo, 1980)	207
29	My Favorite Sins (live at CAJE, 1985) (Parody by Cliff Cohen)	

Produced by Jeff Klepper
Engineered and mastered by Dave Lefkowitz
Art direction by Alex Nosevich
Photo credits: Cindy Levitt, Angela Gold, Enid Bloch, Elyse Frishman, Jim Ball
See original releases for additional credits

Snapshots: The Best of Kol B'Seder Volume III (1989–1993)

(CD compilation 2024)

For primary tracklist, see original releases of Sparks of Torah *and* In Every Generation.

Reissue produced by Jeff Klepper
Production help from David Billotti
Art direction by Rick Lupert
Mastering by Eric Kilburn
Photo credits: Steve Goodman, Cindy Levitt, Enid Bloch
See original releases for additional credits

Kol B'Seder Songbooks

Especially Jewish Symbols Songbook

(Published by ARE [Alternatives in Religious Education], Denver, CO, 1977). *Out of print.*

Bible People Songbook

(Published by ARE [Alternatives in Religious Education], Denver, CO, 1981.) *Out of print.*
Listen at kolbseder.com/archives

Yom Chadash Songbook

(Published by the Leo Baeck Education Center, Haifa, Israel, 1988.) *Out of print.*

Songs for Growin'

(Published by ARE [Alternatives in Religious Education], Denver, CO, 1992.) *Out of print.*

The Kol B'Seder Songbook

(Published by Tara Publications, Cedarhurst, NY, 1996.) *Out of print.*

Songs for Growin'

(Reissue published by Transcontinental Music Publications, Schaumburg, IL, 2002.)

Jeff Klepper Anthology: Shabbat Evening Music

(Published by Transcontinental Music Publications, Schaumburg, IL, 2011.)

Includes 26 liturgical songs, most with keyboard accompaniment

Notable compilation songbooks including Kol B'Seder songs:

Yehi Shir: Let There Be Song (1981)

Shaarei Shirah: Gates of Song (1987)

NFTY's Fifty Songbook (1989)

Complete Jewish Songbook for Children: Manginot
Volume I (1991), *Volume II* (2004), and *Volume III* (2021)

Shireinu series
Shireinu Chordster (2000)
The Complete Shireinu and *The Complete Jewish Songbook*
Volume I (2001) and *Volume II* (2025)
Shireinu Songbook (words only) (2001)

Ruach: New Jewish Tunes series
5761 (2001), *5763* (2003), *5775* (2015)

R'fuah Sh'leimah: Songs of Jewish Healing (2002)

The Complete Chanukah Songbook (2003)

Shabbat Anthology series
Volume I (2003), *Volume II* (2004), and *Volume III* (2005)

URJ Biennial Songbook series
2003, *2009*, and *2017*

Torah Alive! Music Connection (2005)

Chazak V'ematz: Jewish Songs of Protest and Hope (2018)

High Holy Days Anthology series
Volume I (2020) and *Volume II* (2023)

Kol Han'shamah: Choir and *Kol Han'shamah: Band*
Volume I (2020) and *Volume II* (2024)

Mikraei Kodesh: Music for Life Cycle and Sacred Moments Volume II (2023)

All selections published by Transcontinental Music Publications

Published choral arrangements of Kol B'Seder songs:

Shalom Rav (arr. Stephen Richards, William Dreskin) (1989)

Oseh Shalom (arr. Stephen Richards) (1990)

Yeish Kochavim (There Are Stars) (arr. Andrea Jill Higgins) (2000)

Mah Tovu (arr. Andrea Jill Higgins) (2001)

Oseh Shalom (arr. Joshua Jacobson) (2008)

Shalom Rav (arr. Joshua Jacobson) (2009)

Oseh Shalom (arr. Marshall Portnoy) (2020)

Shalom Rav (arr. Rachelle Nelson) (2024)

Adonai Oz (Y'vareich et Amo) (arr. Dave Schlossberg) (2024)

Modim Anachnu Lach (arr. Dave Schlossberg) (2024)

Shabbat HaMalkah (arr. Eleanor Epstein) (2024)

Yism'chu (arr. Dave Schlossberg) (2024)

All selections published by Transcontinental Music Publications

Audio Track List for Accompanying Album

Track Title	*Track Number*	*Track Title*	*Track Number*
Abraham	1	Hanitzanim	34
Adon Olam	2	Haporeis Sukkat Shalom	35
Adonai, Adonai	3	Hashiveinu	36
Adonai Oz (Y'vareich et Amo)	4	Healing Prayer (Adonai Y'vareich)	37
Af, Peh, Ozen (Parts of My Body)	5	Hineih Mah Tov Blues	38
Again and Again (*Amidah* for Children)	6	Hodo al Eretz	39
Ahavah Rabbah	7	Hold Fast to Dreams (The Bridge)	40
Al Sh'loshah D'varim I (HaOlam Omeid)	8	I Will Plant for My Children (Honi's Song)	41
Al Sh'loshah D'varim II (HaOlam Kayam)	9	Ilu Finu	42
Aleinu	10	Im Ein Ani Li	43
Anah Halach Dodeich	11	I'm Growin'	44
Another Year, Another Chanukah	12	In Every Generation (B'chol Dor Vador)	45
Ashrei	13	In the Beginning	46
Ashrei Adam Matza Chochmah	14	In This Place	47
Ashreinu	15	Jeff's Nigun	48
Avinu Malkeinu	16	Jonah	49
Baruch She-amar	17	Ki Anu Amecha	50
Bayom Hahu	18	The Kippah Song	51
The Bimah Song	19	K'shoshanah	52
B'sefer Chayim	20	Laasok B'divrei Torah	53
Chanukah Lights	21	Lailah Tov	54
Chatzi Kaddish	22	Lamdeini Elohai (Teach Me to Pray)	55
Chazak, Chazak	23	L'chah Dodi	56
Coming Home	24	L'chu N'ran'nah	57
Cowboy Jew from Mars	25	Leidah Hi Reishit (Birth Is a Beginning)	58
Eichah Ashir	26	Lirdof Tzedek (Blessing for Social Justice)	59
Eilu D'varim	27	Lo Alecha	60
Elohim Y'choneinu (Psalm 67)	28	Lo Bashamayim Hi	61
Empty Chair	29	Maariv Aravim	62
Esa Einai	30	Mah Tovu	63
Give Me Sleep (Hashkiveinu)	31	The Mezuzah Song	64
Halomeid	32	Mi Amar	65
Haneirot Halalu	33	Mi Chamochah	66

Boston Jewish Music Festival concert, The Rashi School, Dedham, Massachusetts, March 15, 2011. (Photograph by Ilan Fisher)